Reflections
from the
Wilde Side

Tam e. Polzer

Dedication

This book goes to everyone who has issues,
so … to everyone.

Acknowledgements

I am truly grateful for my children Alois and Eva and my husband, Robert. Their sharp wits and talents never cease to amaze me. I thank my life-time friend and chief editor, Greg DiSanto, as well as Sara Dobie Bauer (author of The Escape Trilogy), Gretchen Reed, Robin Keever, Mary Dregne, members of my writers' groups (Scribble Maniacs, Water's Edge, and The Inklings), and my spiritual book club gals for providing feedback at various stages of my project. I appreciate Tracy Baranauskas, dear friend and fabulous life coach, for her encouragement in writing this book and Cheri Kropac (Locked on Point Photography) for shooting my about the author photo. I honor authors Pema Chödrön, Neale David Walsch, and Caroline Myss for their inspiration and spiritual guidance, and I respect the National Alliance for Mental Illness (N.A.M.I.) for its informational classes and available support for those in need.

Contents

Contents

Contents

Contents

Although this is mostly all true for the Wilde family,
it could just as easily be true for me and you.

The Broom, the Box, the Bedroom Closet

Looking back, I should have known something was up before I married my husband. "Just keep a long-handled broom around, so whenever he gets out of line, it'll be handy to hit him with. That's how I dealt with him," is what my mother-in-law told me before I married her son.

"Aaahhh, he'll settle down when he gets to be about 50. That's how long it took for Daddy, right?" said the oldest sister.

"His apartment is like a museum, ya know," said the second oldest. "And everything has to be perfect, *is* perfect, or he'll freak. And believe me, you don't wanna see him freak."

"Oh, beware of the box," said the third born. "If things aren't where they belong, he'll throw them into the box, and if things aren't taken out of the box and put away within twenty-four hours, he'll throw them out—he's got some serious OCD issues."

The fourth sister added, "You must be crazy to want to marry my brother. Don't get me wrong. I love him to death, but I'd never, ever in a million years choose to live with him. I'd probably have to kill him if I did. But if you do go through with it, for God's sake, don't breed. The world doesn't need more crazies like him."

"When I was seven and Leo was five," said the fifth, "he convinced me to jump off of the garage roof with him while holding an umbrella. He promised we could fly. I'm surprised we didn't die. He always loved doing crazy things like that. When we would stare at him, aghast, he would say something like, 'What's the big dang dilly deal?'"

And the sixth and youngest sister said, "Our bedroom was a closet—we had just enough room for our bunk beds. And a shelf for his German model tank collection. Maybe that's why he's a little cuckoo—like Grandpa." She twirled her finger up by her head.

My husband was the seventh child and only boy. With that history alone, many of our friends predicted potential marital problems. But I thought, "Wow. I am in love with the coolest, funniest, most creative, athletic, motivated, talented, and smartest to the point of genius-kind-of guy in the universe. His six sisters and mom must be crazy in the head."

It turns out they weren't, but I probably was. I married him.

Wilde Mind

I was named Katarina Trula in honor of my great-grandmother. But everyone calls me K.t. My maiden name is Geist, and I married Leonard Rudolf Wilde, whom I fondly call Leo. In German, Geist means "mind or spirit" and Wilde means "wild." I never really thought about the equation our marriage made, until it was too late.

$$\text{Wilde} + \text{Geist} = \text{Wild Mind or Spirit}$$

There it was—*another* sign—waving like a red flag in a blue sky, but I didn't even think about it. I was in love with a man I'd admired forever, and I was flying high. In fact, my high school students thought I *was* high, because I was walking on cloud nine throughout our six month courtship, one week engagement, and the beginning of our marriage. I couldn't wipe the smile off my face.

But, as you all know, math doesn't lie, and before long, I was on the Wilde Ride.

Wilde Ride

I don't know if people can understand what it's like dealing with mental illness and addiction unless they personally experience them or live with others who do. I don't know how to describe the intensity of the journey, but a rollercoaster ride with manic highs and dark lows and unpredictable twists may work for now. I'm not saying all passengers are always holding on for dear life, but I still wouldn't wish the ride upon anyone—especially my eclectic, artisan husband and my creative, wise children.

In this collection, I left out some details to protect the ones I love (if that's even possible) and specific dates because they don't matter. Although the ten year chaotic ride blurred my mind so gaps and out-of-order sequences exist, my hope is that each piece, read in any order, may help people gain insight into not only mental illness and addiction, but also relationships, spirituality, and even ghosts. In addition, I pray readers will stop feeling so alone and/or find hope on this wild ride we call life.

One more thing: we all have issues, no matter who we are, so let's remember … with acceptance, forgiveness, and love … we might have a smoother ride.

K.t. and Leo

Ten couples bet on if Leo and I would make it through a year of marriage. Nine to one bet against us. And I know why. Simply put, it was a safe bet. After all, our marriage did start off in hell. Even though everybody liked both of us because we had hearts as wide as the horizon and would do about anything for anybody, nobody, and I mean nobody, could imagine us making a marriage last. We were just too opposite. I saw every shade of gray; Leo, only black and white. Sure, opposites attract and all, but please. How could such a free-spirited, "if-you-can't-say-anything-nice-don't-say-anything-at-all" kind of girl live peacefully with a perfectionist "if-they-can't-take-the-truth-that's-their-problem" kind of guy? And vice-versa.

Even though we're both dedicated (I taught high school English for thirty years and he still owns his own carpentry business); even though we both love music (he plays drums and I play guitar); and even though we both love nature (he loves sleeping in a snowdrift in -10 degree snowstorms and I love hiking in the autumn woods on a 60 degree day), as I said, our marriage *did* start off in hell.

After a seven day engagement, my neighbor and dear friend, Reverend Paul, married us on a cold and snowy morning in a metro park in which we fell in love. That's when all hell broke loose. You see, Leo came from a strict, Catholic family and was supposed to be married in a church by a priest to a nice Catholic girl. But I wasn't Catholic. I came from an easy-going family who practiced the old adage of "Love one another." I was supposed to be married on my parents' front lawn under the weeping willow tree as did my older sisters and not steal the pride away from the mother of the bride who wanted to help by planning everything. But my mom couldn't even help me pick out my wedding gown because I didn't wear one. I wore a cotton sweater, Levi jeans, and cowboy boots, because I wanted to keep it inexpensive. After all, I was broke, still paying off my college loans. Besides, my parents were retired. Leo, who calls himself a "cheap bastard," wore his black, wool sweater, Levi jeans, and combat boots, because he wished to forgo all of the who-haw that goes along with tying the knot--after all, he was a country boy.

He wanted to keep it simple. So, he asked me to marry him the day after my dad told him to "shit or get off the pot." (I had stayed overnight at Leo's place on a Saturday night, and my dad was *not* happy). A week later we got married on Monday morning at 9:00 a.m. by the treacherous ravine with a golden glow in the park where we fell in love called Hell's Gold.

Anyways, with God, nature, and a few family members who could take off work at such short notice as our witnesses, we were officially married. Hence, the marriage that started in Hell began and the bets started flying.

Leo developed habits from his workaholic, military father; I from my project-loving, caretaking mom. Always being in the go-go mode, we had a hard time relaxing, especially after we had kids.

Initially, neither of us wanted kids. Leo watched the life be sucked out of all six of his sisters after kids came along. He saw their households become chaotic and his sisters' freedom usurped by butts with rashes, bottles, burps, blankets, binkies and little twerps. He did *not* want to see that happen to me. I didn't want kids for the longest time either, because what if they turned out like some of my high school students--ornery, angry and having no respect for themselves or any authority? Anyways, after five years of marriage, the world welcomed Aries, our bright, blue-eyed son, and before the blur cleared, Lavender, our artsy, beautiful daughter. Both kids had colic and screamed for six months straight. Leo and I screamed at each other. Our house, under major reconstruction, screamed to be completed. We lived in our barn when we tore off the roof of our farm house and built on, up and out, which put both of us over the edge. There weren't enough hours in the day to raise two kids, work full-time, and live comfortably in the constant chaos of a construction site. Leo freaked, finding no order in sight; and I, exhausted, couldn't make things right.

Leo *needed* everything to be in its place, and he had a place for everything. He could succinctly tell anyone how to retrieve anything:

"Go to the north east corner of the barn. Look on the third shelf from the bottom. Find the fifth coffee can from the right. Bring me two square head bolts." He became frustrated if a thing like the attachment to the shop vac wasn't where it was supposed to be. I would rather retrieve it myself than try to explain that "It may be hidden under the blanket beneath the book bag beside the stack of bills to be paid, or it may be inside the dryer because Aries was using it as a magic wand and he hid it there, or, hmmm, maybe it's with that to-be-put-away pile in the garage."

Although I couldn't always maintain perfect order, I could multi-task to cope with the chaos and diligently deal with the day-to-day that my husband couldn't. Although Leo couldn't always maintain his cool, he could focus on one task at a time until its fruition. He had experience in every trade. He worked magic with his hands, turning everything he touched into something beautiful, including changing our dilapidated farmhouse into a castle.

Yes, we certainly were different. We've always been different. In high school, Leo spent hours trying to blow dry his curly hair straight while I spent hours in hot rollers for the Farrah Fawcett look. He was teased for his chicken legs and knobby knees; I, for my thunder thighs and bubble butt. Even today, he is the night owl, lover of music and wood-working tools; I, the early bird, lover of silence and words. His emotions run rampant. He says what's on his mind at the moment. He has been nicknamed "un-schedulable Leo," because he's unable to commit to anything unless it's work related because of his capricious nature. I stay calm and collected, analyzing everything before I speak, and I am predictable, hence dubbed, "Steady Betty." He complains that he still can't grow a beard at 50-something; I complain that my tweezers can't keep up with my mustache and the black hairs growing out of my chin. He says people should *always* finish *all* of their work before play; I say there's *no* possible way. According to our children's friends, I was the Kool-Aid mom and Leo, the meanest dad in the neighborhood.

K.t. and Leo (Continued)

Yes. We are very opposite. But the main reason people bet we wouldn't make it--the fact that I am the free-spirited, "if-you-can't-say-anything-nice-don't-say-anything-at-all" kind of girl and Leo is the perfectionist, "if-they-can't-take-the-truth-that's-their-problem" kind of guy is the reason we stay together. He craves my free-spirit and loves my positive energy, although sometimes it really pisses him off. I appreciate his perfectionism and to-the-point language, although sometimes it's overwhelming and hurtful. He's learned to ease up, get a grip; I've learned to nip things in the bud and delegate. We've grown to respect each other immensely, despite our differing, deep-seated beliefs and the challenging heartaches we've faced. Ironically, we're still together, although the nine couples that bet against us aren't.

I'm not saying we don't have rough times, because we do. I'm not saying we like each other all of the time, because we don't. But somehow, some way, we amaze each other and many along the way with our crazy combination of move forward with patience and compassion, look backwards with empathy and respect, and move forward with admiration and love. We believed in each other and won the bet, although the odds were against us.

But nobody said a marriage starting off in hell would be easy, now did they?

Shattered Lives (Mom)

I didn't know
so   much of life   would
crack   m e   in half.   Being
s h a t t e r e d   into   sl iv

ers   unable   to be delivered in one   piece,

creates havoc in my soul.   Concentrating on

one   shard   at   a   time

is not so hard, but trying to   put all the pieces where they

go   overwhelms,   slows me down,

tears m e up, and cuts me deeply,   yet,

I know

Each   s
         h
          at
         t
          er
           e
          d
piece
         weeps   silently,

searching
         for
   hope.
         So I   keep on   trying.

Shattered Lives (Son)

I am the new generation—
Generation X.
My body is built for drugs,
and my consciousness is
beyond all that you see.
I hate people
who are pussies,
and I don't care what anyone thinks,
because nobody knows what I'm going through,
and nobody cares about me.

Shattered Lives (Dad)

What is all of this debris? Why aren't things where they belong? I can't take it anymore. There's too much going on. Too much! Why is there always so much confusion? I can't fucking take it. I'm done. Where's the gun?

Shattered Lives (Daughter)

All I did was sleep. Then I didn't sleep for weeks. When I finally did, I had this nightmare. I dropped this glass of water and it shattered all over the kitchen floor. When I leaned over to pick it up, I fell down. My hands and knees landed in the glass. I kept pulling out shard after shard. The pieces that I pulled out kept getting longer and longer. And then I was eating the glass and blood was everywhere. Then I didn't sleep again for weeks.

Leonard: "Why isn't there any gas in your car? My truck took a shit yesterday and I need to borrow your car and get the hell out of here and go to work. What kind of person leaves their tank that low?"

K.t: *Hmmm. I was planning on getting gas when I went for groceries today. How was I supposed to know his truck died and he needed mine if he never told me?*

Aries and K.t: "Do you have any idea of what that does to me physiologically? Everyday waking up to that … bitching?

"It's certainly not every day, but yeah, I—"

"No, you don't. You don't have a clue. Energy comes and goes, but memory sticks. Cell memory. From way back. Since I was a kid, he's taken his alpha energy out on me."

"Yes, I do have a clue. I have lived with him for years and have learned to not take his bitching personally. He's just venting—he's not mad at you. He's frustrated that he has to get gas and that wasn't in his vision."

"You're not seeing the big picture, bitch."

"You don't like to hear bitching and I don't like to be called 'bitch.' I'll talk to you later when you can be nice to me."

Lavender and K.t: "Mom! Why didn't you wake me up? You gotta be kidding! Why didn't you wake me up?"

"I have been waking you up every fifteen minutes for an hour and a half. I pulled blankets off you and I shook you. You kept saying, 'Give me fifteen more minutes.'"

"What the heck? You can't believe me when I say that. I'm still sleeping when I say that! Now I'm gonna be late for cross-country practice. You shoulda tried harder."

"What else do you want me to do? Why don't you set your own alarm and be responsible for waking yourself up? You're fifteen, for God's sake."

"Why are you yelling at me? I *do* set my own alarm. For three different times. But it's hard to wake up at 8 a.m. when I don't fall asleep until 6 a.m."

Five minutes later:

"Bye, Mom. I'm going to Jason's. We're gonna make a movie. Have a superlative day," said Aries, giving his mom a swift kiss on her cheek …

Ten minutes later:

"Mommy, you're the best," said Lavender, giving her mom a quick hug …

Ten hours later:

"Hi, Dear. Wow, what a day!" said Leo, giving his wife a full body embrace …

… as if nothing had happened earlier …

Commitment, Responsibility, Promises Were Made

Why don't you just go?
Get your face out of this hornet's nest and go.

Why don't you just go? You're the one who's so angry.

Because I can't. I made a commitment.
Promises were made.
I have to be responsible for the bed I made.
Since I have to stay, my price to pay
is cleaning up the mess of my life you've made.
Remember, you're the one who wanted children
and to live in the city,
knowing I'd rather be "the uncle" enjoying country living,
so I'm dealing with resentfulness, tightness in my chest, and I
hate it when you can't see the obvious.

*Oh, so the reason you won't leave is because
you have to keep a promise you made years ago
despite that we've evolved and nothing new has been solved
and we're both still so miserable?*

Don't you get it?
Commitment. Responsibility. Promises were made.
I can't ignore that, although it seems a waste.

*We are too good to waste away.
I say to hell with commitment,
responsibility, and promises made.
The last thing I ever wanted to do was trap you,
wrap you up in a world you never wanted,
by forcing you to be a dad and
moving to the city with sidewalks.*

Commitment, Responsibility, Promises Were Made (Cont.)

I've told you over and over
we'd be better off as friends,
but your response every time was
"Commitment. Responsibility. Promises were made."
Which is not ok, when you're so resentful
you can't sleep at night,
feel so guilty that you're being eaten alive,
and are so angry that you take things out on me
for decisions you made to acquiesce and please.
So, please ... leave. Leave me for your sanity,
and for the kids' and my sake.
You can blame it all on me, like you do anyways.

It's too late. I can lay awake all night
wishing I were in a different place,
a different time, *wishing* I could unwind
my life and find the path leading to the place where
I was free to be before we married.
But it won't change anything. Because of
commitment, responsibility, and promises made.
I'd lose my honor as a man if I caved.

But, what is so honorable about keeping a promise
when it makes you so unhappy
and everything has changed?
You could have said no to the kids and the city
and stuck to your guns without self-pity,
and I could have made a decision to adapt and stay
or been the bad guy and gone, tossing away
commitment, responsibility and the promises made.
We both could have started over before we even began.
You didn't say no, so I didn't go.
But if I had known that you'd throw in my face
all of your "I told you so's" every single day
I would've gone. My heartache would've faded ...

Commitment, Responsibility, Promises Were Made (Cont.)

I wouldn't be dealing with your mood swings—
their twists and turns--
your complicated OCD, stabbing, angry words,
days of only silence,
a tightness in my chest,
your eating disorder, aching body,
insomnia, and resentfulness.
I try to help you with your anxiety,
but you push me away.
You know how much I love you, but
you're right. I just can't stay.

Honey, I'm sorry. Although I'm a pretty smart guy,
when my mind races, my mouth spews words,
I can't control it--I don't know why.
I'm actually embarrassed of my actions.
I can't believe the things I say.
I can't sleep. I'm going crazy.
Please, please don't go away.

Well, you won't take any medicine--
say you'd rather suffer and live in pain.
I try and respect your wishes, but what do I have to gain
when you're growling like an angry bear
trapped in the madness of your mind somewhere?
Besides, after all these years together
when I've reached my end, can't cope,
you always tell me to walk away—
say that's my only hope.

I never mean to hurt you with things I say and do.
You're the best thing in my life and you know that's true.

Commitment, Responsibility, Promises Were Made (Cont.)

My skin is only so tough.

But you're the only one I love.

And you're the only one I love.

So, please.
Do what you need to do
to make your heartache fade.

Ok.
I'm leaving.
I'm gonna take the kids to Gramma's.
We'll be back in a few days,
because after all…
Commitment,
Responsibility,
and Promises were made.

I took Aries to a mental health assessment last week because the school highly suggested that I take him. I guess he went on a rant saying everyone has the divine within and some teachers and students freaked out. Well, the assessment counselor made him leave because he thought he was on drugs, but Aries swore he wasn't. He seemed his normal, weird self to me. So I took him again today and Aries liked the guy who will be working with him. Aries said he felt "all of this energy in his head and didn't know what to do with it." He said he didn't want to do anything but think so he could "figure out ways to manifest" what he needs.

I can't talk to Leo about any of this because he's mad at the school for forcing Aries to get involved in the mental health system again. So, I keep it all inside. No wonder I can't breathe. I want to do some yoga to help me relax, but I don't have time because I have to grade papers every night to keep up, and then I'm watching shows I don't like to hang out with Leo and staying up too late to hang out with the kids. I'm doing everything for everyone else and never anything for myself, and I can't even say what's on my mind. At least Leo and Aries and Lavender say what's on their mind. I need to learn from Aries how to "figure out ways to manifest" what I need.

"What are you gonna do differently next time, so you don't get kicked out of school again?"

"Stay away from anybody who says something like, 'If you jump over the railing from the 2nd floor to the 1st floor in the school you'll die.' Because then I'll just have to jump."

"Can't you just leave it alone when you know that you can do it?"

"*No*. No no no no *no*! You don't understand. I *can't* let something like that go."

"But you have to--to get through school. To get through life. You can't prove people wrong every time they say something out loud that challenges you."

"But I do. And I will. And that's all there is to it. I'm not going to let people think I'm some kind of pussy."

"People don't think that about you. And some don't know that you have no fear and are so agile that you *can* jump from 2nd floors to 1st floors without getting hurt."

"Everybody knows that I do back flips and crazy shit and not get hurt."

"Obviously not everybody. The teacher that turned you in at school thought you were trying to kill yourself."

"*What?*"

"She had no clue that you did a back flip off the second floor railing to prove to a friend that it was a piece of cake for you. It scared the hell out of her. You have to know that your actions affect other people."

"Only if they're pussies."

"Well, I was scared shitless that time I saw you run off of the school's roof and do a backflip in the air before landing in the pricker bushes. Especially when you came out all bloody."

"That was nothing."

"To you. To me it was horrifying."

"That's because you're a girl."

"No. It's because I'm a human being with feelings."

"Why do you care so much? I wish you didn't care so much."

18

"I can't help it that I'm a mom."

"My friends' moms don't care so much. They don't give a shit, and I think that's way better than the way that you are."

"I am what I am."

"Well, I am what I am, too. So why don't you just accept it and get off my back?"

"I'm not on your back. We're just talking."

"You just piss me off whenever I'm around you. You always want to talk about it."

"I'm just hoping you're learning from your actions. You tell me you have to experience things before you can learn. So did you learn anything?"

"Yeah. That lady who turned me in is a pussy."

All Symptoms Go

When Aries brought these lists home from health class, I gave them to each member of my family. All three said, "They're all me" for the Depression symptoms. For the Bipolar, they each checked all symptoms except for the last three. Go figure. How do I prepare for blast off?

Depression Symptoms

Persistent sad, anxious or "empty" mood
Loss of interest or pleasure in ordinary activities
Feelings of hopelessness, pessimism, helplessness
Change of appetite or weight
Decreased energy, fatigue, "slowed down" feeling
Restlessness and irritability, increased anger
Decreased ability to concentrate, remember
Inability to make decisions
Headaches or stomach issues
Thoughts of death, suicide, or wishes to be dead

Bipolar Disorder Symptoms

Increased energy, activity, restlessness
Racing thoughts and rapid talking
Excessive "high" or euphoric feelings
Decreased need for sleep
Significant risk-taking
Extreme irritability and distraction
Sustained periods of unusual, even bizarre behavior
Unrealistic beliefs in one's abilities and powers (grandiosity)
Denial that anything is wrong

Advocate for Typical

September 15

Hello, Miss K. I wanted to tell you I appreciate the lesson you gave about bipolar/depression yesterday. I'm wondering if you did it on purpose since it was such good timing for Aries. When he went to his psychiatrist yesterday, Aries showed the doctor the list you gave your students. He checked off all the symptoms that pertained to him and said he never saw everything on one list before. Now he realizes that he probably does need the meds after listening to kids in the movie say they, too, tried not taking their meds, but soon realized they needed them. The doctor said it is *typical* for patients to purposely go off of their medication to see how they feel, searching for normal, but not really knowing what normal is.

You have gone above and beyond with trying to help Aries, and my husband and I appreciate your patience. Aries is willing to try medicine again even though he had a serious rash with the last one he tried. The doctor is assuring him that with patience he can find the right mix although there are always side effects.

Anyways, since all of this has happened, as my son's advocate, I'd like him to be able to make-up the school work he missed when he was suspended for jumping off of the 2nd floor stair case railing. I'd like to talk with you more about this, so please call when you have a chance.

Thank you, Katarina Wilde

Space to Be

She stood and stared at the stars.
Energy flowed through her bones.
Autumn night awed her and although
alone
she felt company,
embraced by a human race
that did not rush,
that did not waste,
but made space
for her to breathe,
believe,
Be
...

My neighbor couldn't believe what Leo did when I was gone with the kids for the weekend. He called Leo a machine because he gutted the entire second story of the house and built all of the new walls alone. My neighbor said the light never went out and Leo worked throughout both nights. I'm not surprised. He does stuff like this all of the time. Last Monday when I was at work, he dug out the entire back yard by hand and put in railroad ties for tiered flower beds and a stone walkway. He can't help himself. He says keeping busy helps him deal with the million thoughts always racing around in his head. Leo should have his picture in the dictionary next to the word "Diligent." Despite extreme heat, cold, hunger, thirst, or severe body aches, he never stops until the job is done. I love to see his joy when working on a project. What makes me sad is that I know his body can only endure so much and his up-beat mood can only last so long. Before ya know it, manic mode will morph and he'll be on the couch, depressed as hell, unable to do a damn thing, waiting and wishing for it all to be over.

The Line

A *fine* line--
A feather-light line lies between pairs:
Insanity/sanity;
Enabling/helping;
Craziness/creative genius.

A **thick** line--
A heavy, black line lies between
Stress/peace.

I want to cross to the other side
of both lines—
the thick, the fine--

Or do I?

Something—some kind of comfort zone?—keeps me where I am.

Maybe I need to make a plan.

A leap of faith?

With faith
I understand
I can cross
the line
any time.

Jump!
?

Oh … breathe   Saturday, January 20

I took Lavender to another assessment today. When asked what year it was, she said, "I have no idea." The counselor said she is concerned about her memory and believes she has signs of Post-Traumatic Stress Disorder. My poor girl. The counselor gave me a referral to someone more qualified to help her, but I can't get an appointment for another three weeks.

So, I'm gonna keep lying down with Lavender every night until she falls asleep. I know Leo gets mad because he misses his time with me, but I need to do what I want to do and that is help my girl. What else can I do?

Oh … breathe. Yeah, breathe.

Fears Exposed

Doctor: "Tell me about the voices."

Lavender: "One time I was sitting in math class and all of a sudden I hear this screaming. Somebody's screaming at me. I look around the room and realize nobody else hears it. I think it's all going on inside my head. I start to freak out and wonder if I'm actually shaking for real. I realize I am, but nobody sees. I push down on my legs to stop them from shaking but the screams won't stop so I can't stop shaking."

Doctor: "Tell me about the visuals."

Daughter: "I don't really see anybody in particular. It's just a figure and he's staring at me from behind a tree or in the mirror's reflection or beside my bed. I'm certain he's going to kill me. And I always imagine hands coming out of drains and yanking me down and suffocating me.

Screaming in her head, a person going to murder her, hands suffocating …

Even after hearing all of those fears pouring out of her, on the way home I left her in the car alone when it was dark and rainy to run into the store for milk and bread. She couldn't stop shaking all the way home and into the night. Damn. I'm such a terrible mother. A stupid schmuck. I should have never let her be alone. I hate this feeling. I hate seeing her suffer … Damn it all.

Need for Speed

March 28

Your Honor:

George Walkman was pulled over for speeding on March 25th.

Having dated my daughter for over a year, he knows her history and when she started having a panic attack in the movie theatre, he sped home with her so she could take her medicine. He witnessed her having to go the emergency room before because of her condition, and he was trying to avoid that.

I thought you might want to take this into consideration before making your judgement.

Sincerely,

Katarina Wilde

Leo interrupts me while I'm scrubbing the shower.

"For God's sake, ya gotta quit coddling the kids. You're not doing them any favors by rescuing them all of the time. How are they ever gonna grow up to be successful adults when you keep babying them? They need to learn to toughen up and be able to cope with shit and they need to be *pushed*. How will they survive in the real world if they can't even handle the easy jobs they have around here? Stop doing their work. Let them suffer through some pain. That's what will help them grow."

"I'm helping them because I know you expected the work to be done, but they both have doctor appointments today and we planned to swim at their cousins later on."

"Every time you take the kids to the doctors for prescription drugs you give them another crutch to stand on. I told the boy to push mow the grass because he let it go too long and I knew it would be tough. I told the girl to scrub the shower and walls in the bathroom because you obviously don't have time and I knew it would be tough. They need to learn if they slack on their everyday jobs they will eventually have to pay the price of working harder. It's a good lesson. But you let them get away with not completing all the work by giving them a hand. I hate it when you undermine my decisions. Am I that bad of a father?"

"You're just so harsh. Can't you even say hello to them first thing in the morning instead of yelling orders to clean the house? Everything can't always be in perfect order, especially when we're renovating. Besides, we had already made plans for the day. I told them I wanted them to empty their book bags, clean up their rooms, vacuum, dust, and match socks before we left for their appointments and headed to go swimming at their cousins. For God's sake, it's 92 degrees, the first day of their summer vacation, and they've been looking forward to this for weeks."

"I'm trying to instill in them that work comes before play."

"I'm trying to instill in them that if we work together the jobs go faster. And I'm taking them to the doctors so they can get a grip on their issues that inhibit them from always being able to do their jobs. Can't you just accept the fact that they have issues? Of all people, I'd think you'd be able to understand what they're going through and have some empathy."

"Yeah, I have issues, too, but I suck it up. You don't see me running to the doctors every time things get tough, do you?"

"No. I just see you freak the fuck out."

"And? At least I'm not taking a bunch of medicine that's helping out no one but the pharmaceutical companies. The kids just have to learn to suck it up."

"But they aren't you. Just because you can suck it up doesn't mean they have the ability to do the same."

The bathroom door slams.

Spirit, Come Back to Me (Song Lyrics)

Spirit, you're my architect—
my heart and soul you build, protect.
Guide me in thoughts I select. Help me truly resurrect.
Spirit, Spirit, Spirit, oh, Spirit.

When I unplug from negativity, you send me needed energy.
When I don't judge but I have mercy and love with no agenda,
I feel free to find God's peace and harmony inside of me.

Spirit, come back to me. Spirit, please set me free
to be the me I'm meant to be,
to find the me I've left behind.

When I believe Thy will be done on Earth as it is in Heaven,
when I release my need to know, forgive, and learn to let go,
with true faith in you I'll grow.

Spirit, come back to me. Spirit, please set me free
to be the me I'm meant to be,
to find the me I've left behind.

You've taught me that All is One,
honor myself, honor everyone,
seek only the Truth, know Love is Divine,
and live in the present time.
How can I leave you behind? How can I leave you behind?

Spirit, what you give to me is everything I need to be
to find the me I'm meant to be—to be the me I've left behind.

Spirit, you're my architect—
my heart and soul you build, protect.
Guide me in thoughts I select. Help me truly resurrect.

Spirit, Spirit, Spirit, Oh, Spirit.
Come back to me.

Kids are like trees   _Sunday, July 10_

Leo told me kids are like trees. If they are straying, you chain, force, and bind them; it's not pretty, but soon enough they turn into beautiful, straight trees. He also said he should have beaten Aries straight years ago, but I wouldn't let him, so now everybody is paying. Me, him, Aries, society…

… I just can't relate to beating a kid to get results. I wasn't brought up that way. I never saw it. But Leo said it's been going on for hundreds of years because it works for the Wilde boys. It worked for him, his father, his father's father, etc., and it's the only way to get results.

Whatever … I just don't have a beating in me to give to anyone, unless it's a beating heart.

Booze and a Broken Heart

My dad died from two things:
booze and a broken heart.
He drank himself to death
cuz he missed Mom so much.

He couldn't face the fact that she was gone,
so he drank and drank
and drank some more
for breakfast from a coffee cup
for lunch from a tumbler with ice
for dinner from a wine glass
for night caps straight from the bottle.

I hid his keys, poured out the booze I found
in the dirty clothes hamper and trunk of his car,
washed his pissed on pants, and wiped up blood
from his head which hit
the corner of the coffee table
when he fell down
stone drunk.

I prayed every time before I opened his door
that I wouldn't find him dead.

Booze and a Broken Heart (Continued)

His broken heart and its alcohol accomplice
took their good old time in knocking him off.
Unlike hired assassins who'd work quickly and cleanly
and escape without a trace,
they did a hack job,
making a mess or every inch of him before finishing,
leaving hard evidence in every heart that loved him.

Pitiful doesn't even come close.

I miss him.
I miss philosophizing in our living room
on the blue couch in front of a soft, burning fire.
I miss cutting his hair while he cried,
sharing stories about Mom.
I miss giving him "toll bridge" kisses
on puckered lips when I passed by.
I miss hearing him tell me and others his favorite sayings:
"Treat others as you'd like to be treated,"
"Not making a decision is making a decision,"
"Learn to like to learn," and "Life is beautiful."

He gave me life
and loved me to his end,
despite his broken heart
and boozed-up head.

He'll never be dead.

"Look at this crappy job the plumbers did. I could've done better with my eyes closed and my hands tied behind my back. What is this world coming to? People who do jobs this terribly are either lazy or stupid. Those are the only reasons I can see for this shoddy job."

"What about ignorant? Maybe they weren't taught."

"Well, if they're ignorant, they should do some research, ask questions, learn from the best. Ignorance is no excuse in my book."

"Well, sometimes it actually *is* an excuse. I've been asking you to teach me the names of all of your tools and a lesson in how to operate them, so I can better help you renovate this house. But you won't make time to do that."

"If you spent more time observing than coddling the kids you'd know all of that."

"Observation doesn't do it for me. I have to *do* it. I can look and observe but still not know. And when there's tension—and there often is—I'm not absorbing anything. I'm too frazzled to suck it up. I can't learn when I'm frazzled. Nobody can."

"People learn best when they're yelled at. They think, *I don't want to be yelled at again, so I won't make that same mistake.* It's as simple as that."

"In your black and white mind it's that simple. But I am all shades of gray, and I'm telling you it doesn't work for me. Maybe the person doing the plumbing felt nervous like I sometimes do when working with you. Or maybe he was feeling really rushed or maybe he had a million things going on in his head and couldn't concentrate."

"Well, I'm always nervous, rushed, and have a million things rushing through my mind, but I still do a perfect job. But look at this shoddy job they did. I can't trust *anybody* to do a good job *ever.*"

"It looks fine to me."

"It's not even near perfect. It's making me crazy. I'm gonna have to tear it out and do it myself."

"But it works, right? Can't you just walk away and not look at it? It's in the crawl space, so you won't even have to see it."

"You don't get it. I don't have to see it to know it's not right. It will haunt me until it's perfect. I won't be able to sleep at night."

"Wow. I'm sorry you can't let it go."

"Believe me, so am I, but how can I in this case? The pipes aren't parallel. That first one is a 32nd off and the second is a 16th off. It looks like a kindergartener did this work. It's ridiculous. I don't want to fall into the land of acquiescence. Then I'd be like everybody else. Lazy or stupid. Or ignorant. And then I couldn't even stand myself."

"I wish you could find some shades of gray so you could find some peace."

"I like being black and white."

"Alrighty then. I don't know what else to say except good luck with that."

"I don't have time for this shit. I gotta go get the plumbing tools so I can fix something I paid somebody else to do. Fuck."

I love being manic   Saturday, October 16

Lavender accidently ran into me in the hallway this morning. She hadn't slept all night and was running around with a huge stack of laundry, putting clothes away. When I asked her how she was feeling, she rapidly said something like this: "I love being manic. I could pick up a car right now. It's the most amazing thing--feeling so alive and happy. But at the back of my skull, I have this feeling that as high as I am now being manic, I will be that low when the depression kicks in. So, yeah, I'm gonna do whatever I can now, cuz I know this mood's not going to last. I know that I'm gonna be in the dark hole soon, so that's why I don't wanna sleep. I don't ever wanna sleep when I feel this good."

No wonder she doesn't want to take her medicine …

This Isn't a Church (Leo and K.t.)

"If I hear, 'This isn't a church' one more time, I'm leaving the job. I can't just slap something together. Everybody's in such a damn hurry. I want to do the right thing and build things the way they should be built so I can give everything a two hundred year guarantee. But that takes time. And the right tools."

"Everyone has different standards."

"Well, I'm not going to build something if I'm going to be embarrassed to put my name on it. I'd like to do jobs for people who want quality work. I don't want to be associated with a job if it's gonna be crrrrrrrrrap."

"I don't blame you. You have to do what makes you be able to sleep at night."

"Yeah, the right thing."

I feel bad for Leo. He works harder than anyone I know and has so much anxiety when people don't care about quality. People actually get on his case for doing *too* nice of a job. They put pressure on him to let things slide, but he can't because he's such a perfectionist. The poor guy can't sleep at night unless the work has been done correctly and is perfect when it's complete. So, he barely *ever* sleeps.

no control

trying, trying, trying, trying
not to think about it but
dwelling, dwelling, dwelling, dwelling,
dwelling, dwelling on it

thinking, thinking, thinking
there's no answer, just a wall
hurting, hurting, hurting, hurting,
hurting are we all

knowing, knowing, knowing, knowing
we have no control over
changing, changing, changing
another person's soul

Dear Aries,   *November 2*

I decided to write you this letter since we can't talk without arguing. Please, read this through—for me, for you.

If you had cancer, surgery, a broken bone, or even the flu, people would go out of their way to help you. They might visit you, send a card, or even bring you homemade chicken soup. But, since you have a chemical imbalance in your brain, people don't know what to say or do to help you feel better. Sometimes they're scared of what they don't understand. That's why they stay away. I don't know exactly what to say or do either, but I do know that I will stand by you, and I won't stop loving you.

After watching the bipolar disorder movie in health class, you know, now, that you're not alone. Other people out there do actually understand what you go through--the madness of mania and the despondency of depression. I'm sure knowing that doesn't make things easier for you, but …

I hope you can remember this disorder is not a sign of weakness, and it's certainly not your fault, so quit blaming yourself. You've beat yourself up long enough. Also, remember there is help out there, so please have faith you can feel better. You're not always going to feel like you do now.

I can only imagine how you must feel. It's hard enough just being a teenager. Especially one living with perfect parents like me and your dad. Ha ha! I know we have high expectations and are always on your case, but we want the best for you. We love you more than you could know.

(Continued)

But now you've been given another challenge to tackle. Why? I don't know. I don't understand why life has to be so hard, especially for the ones I love. However, I'm starting to understand why you acted the way you did. When you were getting suspended from school and fighting with your father, I figured you were beginning your rebellious teenager phase. But, I was puzzled. I knew you loved school and hated missing it. I knew how much you admired your dad and felt tortured if you disappointed him. I couldn't figure out why you kept setting yourself up. Now I know why you did such risky things with no concern of the consequences. Now I know why you had no ability to control your words and actions. Now I know why you had tons of energy or none at all. You couldn't help it that your frontal lobe wasn't filtering things as it should.

I felt so bad for you! A lot of the things you did weren't your fault. I'm so sorry you had such harsh consequences when you couldn't help yourself. No wonder you lashed out so much. No wonder you said you didn't want to live anymore because nobody understood you.

That's why I want to help you with your medicine. The right one or combination can help alleviate those sad, angry, or suicidal feelings. I ask you about your medicine because I care, not because I want to tick you off. I'm not treating you like a baby, as you would say. I'm doing what Grandma does for Grandpa. What Uncle Lou does for Aunt Kristie. What you would do for your best friend. I know you only take your medicine when you think about it. I understand this, because it's new. I want to help you establish a routine because I know that the medicine only works if taken steadily. I want to help monitor your dose so we know what's working and what isn't. That way we can help the doctor find what is right for you.

40

(Continued)

I'm willing to fight with you to fight for you, so you can yell all you want and even hate me if that helps. I'm willing to help you take charge of your illness, so you can move on with your life and reach your dreams.

You are not a lazy, crazy loser, despite what you think. You're a kind-hearted, funny, agile, intelligent guy. You help everyone you meet without asking for anything in return. I want you to know it's not a sign of weakness to accept help from me. I pray we can get through this together.

Hang in there, Aries. You're worth it.

Love and hugs,

Mom

Searching for the Limits

I'm searching for the limits,
trying to find the line,
wondering when to step over,
hoping to stop in time.
Do I wake you up when your alarm's not set
or let you be late when you forget?
Do I remind you to take your medicine and
ask where you're going and where you've been?
Do I force you to be independent?
Is it what you need and want?
Do I push you to your limit or
with your mood swings should I not?
Do I drive you to Doctor S.
for pharmaceutical meds
or do the holistic route and take you to Doctor Ted?
Do I make you food when you're hungry
because that's what "good" moms do?
Am I enabling by helping you manage your life?
Should I leave things up to you?
You're so different every day—
every hour, sometimes minute.
I try to accept and love, but sometimes when I'm in it
my heart hurts.
I lash out.
I want to
find a new route.
So, I'm searching for the limits, trying to find the line
that shows me where to stand to make things right.

Notes on another new medication for Lavender _January 5-16_

Mon.   She was nervous, yet excited for a new start. Cleaned room, couldn't sit down.

Tues.   She was hot and tired … had a panic attack because the laundry was wrinkled.

Wed.   She said "I can deal with odd number hours of sleep better than even numbers." Hmmm …

Thu.   She said, "I think I'm OCD. I have to make a list and if I don't do it in order, I freak out."

Fri.   I picked her up from school because she had a panic attack when kids were talking about blood.

Sat.   She had a panic attack at the school dance so she came home early.

Sun.   She never went to sleep.

Mon.   I stayed home from work to be with her and called the doctor. He said to double her dose.

Tues.   Kids made fun of her for falling asleep in class. She had another panic attack, so the nurse kept her in the clinic until she could walk.

Wed.   Her tongue swelled up in the middle of the night. I took her to the hospital. ER doc prescribed another new medication. She said, "I'm done. I'm not taking any more meds. I'd rather not sleep and have panic attacks than deal with these side effects." I can't blame her.

Thu.   We went to her psychiatrist. He wanted her to try something else. She said she was done with all the bullshit medicine. The doctor gave me the trial packet anyway--just in case she still couldn't sleep and became delusional.

Fri.   She still hasn't slept. She is delirious. She is laughing one minute and then crying the next but still adamant about not taking prescriptions. She rages against me when I'm trying to convince her to try the new prescription. She calls me a pill pusher. That really struck me, because, in truth, I guess I am. I wanted her to do everything holistically, but even the holistic healers give her pills to swallow. Healers scold me for giving her prescription drugs at such a young age and the medical doctors lecture me on messing around with herbal remedies and supplements not fda approved. So, what am I supposed to do? Call the doctor? The hospital? The Healer? The Psychic? The Angels? The frickin' Ghost Busters?!

Could someone please tell me what to do to help my daughter?

Mom and Daughter, 3:30 a.m.

"Honey, besides not being able to sleep, what else is going on? Are you still seeing the negative images in your head?"

"Ah, yeah … because I'm frickin' crazy. Why do you all of a sudden care about my sleep and what's going on? This has been going on for years, so why do you seem to give a damn now?"

"What do you mean? I used to lay down with you every night when you were scared and couldn't sleep. And then I looked into holistic alternatives like reflexology, reiki, massage, and aromatherapy, because I didn't want you to get addicted to prescription drugs. But you weren't interested in trying them."

"Whatever."

"Then we tried three different sleep aids over the counter. Then we went to the doctors and you tried prescriptions. When that didn't work, we tried another holistic approach with Dr. K."

"That quack, you mean."

"You never even gave her a chance. After doing the muscle testing, she gave you four different vitamins with the minerals that *your* body said it was lacking, but you didn't even try them because you said you hated the taste of the pills and said all that "natural" healing stuff is a bunch of BS."

"Mom, all those 'natural healers' are just trying to get your money. You really think they can heal you by doing energy work and clearing your chakras?"

"It's been known to happen."

"You gotta be kidding me, Mom. Then you couldn't let the natural thing go and took me to the freaky "Ooohm" lady who told me to take her crazy concoction —'it help, not hurt,' she said—but it made me have an anxiety attack which made my entire body go numb. Then I was shaking and crying and had to leave school. So much for the natural technique. Do you have any idea how embarrassed that made me?"

"I'm so sorry you had to go through that. That really was bad."

"You have no idea."

"You're right. I don't. I'm so sorry. But I've never stopped trying   to   help."

"Maybe you should stop."

"How can I? I can't stop when you need help. When you asked if you could go back to the first doctor, I took you. She wanted you to go to the sleep clinic. But you didn't want to, so she gave you the anti-anxiety medication."

"Yeah. That stuff made me even worse—I picked at my nails until I bled."

"So she suggested you go to the psychiatrist. And I took you."

"Yeah, and he gave me a medication that finally made me sleep. But then I kept falling asleep during class and I gained twenty pounds. Do you know what it's like to wake up with drool coming out of your mouth in a class filled with kids you don't know who are laughing at you because you slept through the bell? And nobody-- not even the teacher--woke you up or even could wake you up if they tried because you were so sedated? Of course you don't. Do you know what it's like to gain twenty pounds in two months while in high school? Of course you don't 'cuz you're the same weight now that you were in high school. And that other drug he prescribed made my eyes have seizures. Do you know how scary that was? Of course you don't because you've never had eye seizures. So now this psychiatrist wants me to try two different prescriptions that I don't want to take because ... fuck that medicine. I just want to be normal. Why can't I be like everyone else?"

"I don't know, Honey. I'm so sorry."

"Whatever."

"I want to help you but I don't know what to do."

"Get away from me. That's what you can do."

Dear Aries,

I 'm sorry you had to spend your 16th birthday in the hospital. I can't even imagine what that was like to wake up in the intensive care unit. The doctors and nurses are taking very good care of you. From what I understand, you will be transported to the psych ward after you are stabilized.

The nurses said you were asking why you were there—said you didn't remember what happened. The principal and ambulance guys told me you were really angry and sad that Mrs. S. was wrecking your childhood by "taking" your best friend away. They said when you found out Tommy moved to Florida without even saying goodbye you lost it. That's when you started hitting your head against the wall. I'm so sorry you felt that bad to hurt yourself like you did.

I understand your sadness. My best friend moved away in 6th grade and I thought I would die without her. But we still keep in touch, and I'm sure you'll figure out a way to do that with Tommy, too. We'll make plans to visit him this summer. Also, I pray you can stop carrying around all of that anger towards Mrs. S. Life happens and people have to do what they have to do to make a living.

When I saw you in the hospital bed with your head all bandaged up, I thought I was going to lose you. I felt so sad. I pray you feel better soon.

I love you more than you could know.

Mom

Demons inside My Head (Song Lyrics)

I got demons inside my head. I got demons inside my head.
They make me crazy--I want them dead.
They make me crazy--I want them dead.
I slam my head against the red brick wall
to fight the demons and make them fall.
I slam my head against the red brick wall.
My blood blends in—but nothing matters at all cuz

Demons are screamin' … and I'm so pissed.
My head is bleeding … My mind is ripped.
Demons are screamin'… Nothing seems real.
Life's an illusion … There's no emotions to feel.

I'm so empty, empty inside.
All I see are big fat egos so wide.
They can't even fit through the door
to my soul but I don't care anymore cuz

Demons are screamin'… My dad is pissed.
My mom—she's grievin'… My sister's flipped.
Demons are screamin'… I'm so ripped.
For no reason … my mind has tripped.

People say I'm crazy. I know that I am.
But life's an illusion—they don't understand.
I am the elite—the chosen one.
I'll find the answers before my time is done.

Demons think they can tell me what to do.
Well, I got news for them and I got news for you.
I'm in charge now so don't fuck with me.
I have plans and I know I'll succeed.
I have plans and I know I'll succeed.

Demons inside My Head (Continued)

Then I'll look back and laugh at you--
all you arrogant, obnoxious fools--
who don't know how to live in harmony
cuz all you care about is power and money.
All you care about is power and money, cuz your

Demons are screamin'... beggin' for more.
Destroy your demons. You don't need them anymore.
Forget the future. Forget the past.
Live in the moment ... and make it last.

We all have demons. Let's make them die.
Then maybe we can see eye to eye.
Destroy our demons and seek within.
Live in the moment--Don't get stuck where we've been.
Live in the moment--Don't get stuck where you've been.

Demons are screamin' ... beggin' for more.
Destroy your demons. You don't need them anymore.
Forget the future. Forget the past.
Live in the moment ... and make it last ...
Make it last ... Make it last ...

phew!

phew! where do you find the energy to work while trying to hold your family together in this crisis, kt? what a gut-wrenching situation. it doesn't take a genius to see aries has a brain disorder and the chemical imbalance has not been remedied, either by the wrong meds or as i suspect, he hasn't given them the time to work by consistent dosage as prescribed. aries must be as scared as you guys. but he must accept his illness and take responsibility for his recovery. you cannot force him to do that. but that makes his condition even scarier. if he is still smoking pot or using other recreational substances, he isn't letting his meds do their job, thus postponing his recovery even more. it sounds like the school is reaching the end of its tolerance. i would guess the next alternative is extended home-bound instruction. what can you and leonard do? you both know that Aries will not get better until he stays clean and takes his meds as directed for an extended period of time with all the adjustments needed along the line. until he is willing to do that, he is placing himself in jeopardy by his behavior and subjecting all of his loved ones to his endless nightmare. according to your description, it sounds like it's time for another hospitalization to get this straightened out before something more tragic occurs. when tony was in crisis, i remember walking around our house, not knowing what to do, waiting for the next upheaval. going off to teach was a welcome time to get away. but when i got home i usually clinched my teeth when i walked through the doorway and into the storm. i can offer you hope that there are good meds out there but it takes a compliant patient for them to work. i know your pain and understand your dilemma. good luck. feel free to write or call whenever you need to.
we joined an organization called the national alliance for mental illness (nami) to help us deal with tony. you should check it out and take their family to family course. it helped us a lot.
love to you all, marcus

Don't blame myself   Nami support group   Wed., June 10

I took Marcus's advice and joined Nami. I signed up for the
Family-to-Family course and after I'm done with that I'll attend
whatever else they have to offer. I also went to one of their
support group meetings tonight and am glad I went. We had a
good discussion and I wrote down some reminders from the
group.

--Don't blame yourself ... I gotta work on this.
-- It is what it is. Accept it ... What else can I do?
-- You are not alone ... I know that but still feel isolated.
-- Join support groups ... It was nice to talk to people who
        actually understand because they're facing it, too.
-- Make healthy limits/boundaries for people with illness and
        for you ... I think making boundaries is one of my main
        lessons to learn in this lifetime. It's like I have none and I
        get sucked up into a vortex of everyone's intensity which
        drains the life out of me.

The Shark

Lavender: "I walked through the living room and heard on The Discovery Channel that it was shark week. I hate sharks, so I went to my room. But all I kept thinking about was sharks. Over and over again. They kept popping up in my head and no matter what I did-- open my eyes, close my eyes, play music, do homework, or watch comedy--sharks dominated my thoughts. Pretty soon, they're no longer in my head … they're in my bed with mouths wide open, staring at me with their black, evil eyes. And they're yelling at me."

Doctor: "Hmmm. What is this? It's not schizophrenia." There is silence and relief for all. He looks at me. "The problem with diagnosing teens is that they have so much stuff going on in their lives—family relationships, friends, peer pressure, school. Also, another problem is that artistic people like Lavender are so intense with details that they can easily imagine the horror so much better than unartistic people. What's happening is that she's living in the unconscious mind and has absolutely no defenses."

K.t.: "I'm worried that I caused this. With all of the house construction going on—the holes in floors, the exposed walls, undone rooms. I know it's scary for her, and I didn't take her out of the situation—I should have removed her from the construction site."

Doctor: "No. That didn't cause it. And I am not just saying that."

K.t.: "Well, what did?"

Doctor: "Like I said, she's living in the unconscious mind without any defenses, so we're going to have to get her out. That's the tricky part. The brain isn't an easy thing to figure out. Especially with teenagers who have so much constantly changing."

Numbness vs. fear   _Monday, August 2_

I felt so sad when Lavender told me this: "I welcome the numbness. It allows me to function. But at times I welcome fear— like the fear that I'm going to be murdered. Just so I can feel something. Just so I can feel alive."

Please, God, help her feel alive without fear.

Help her feel joy ...

Brain Game

Pushing beyond barriers,
experimenting with the mind,
adding extra doses
to see how things unwind.
The brain game he'll keep playing,
seeking other worlds.
The brain game he'll keep craving,
embracing every swirl.

He thinks he's invincible,
because how things unfold.
He does whatever drugs he can.
For him there is no mold.

I pray he's satisfied
before he goes beyond
whatever is protecting him
before his mind is

gone

...

The Chicken or the Egg?

Many people ask:
Which came first?
The chicken or the egg?

Well, I ask:
Which came first?
The drug abuse or the brain disorder?
At this point, though, I guess it doesn't even matter,
because the drug abuse and the brain disorder
areso
scrambled
together
theyare
one.

Could it be ghosts?   _Friday, September 10_

Could it be ghosts in my house that are making my kids and husband unable to sleep at night? Could ghosts be the cause of their anxiety?

I'm wondering this because while playing my guitar in the back yard today with my back to the house, I suddenly felt extremely paranoid, like I was being watched. It freaked me out and made me really anxious. I wanted to unzip my skin, crawl out of my body, and run. Wow. That never happened to me before. If that's how the kids and Leo feel all of the time-- extremely anxious--no wonder they're so on edge.

Could the lady who died giving child birth in Aries's room many years before we moved in be haunting them? If so, why am I not always being spooked as well?

I don't know. Who am I supposed to talk to about this? Everyone around me at the last nami meeting believed a lady in our support group was kind of coo-coo when she said she thought her son who was diagnosed with schizophrenia needed an exorcism. But if there are angels and guardian spirits protecting us, why can't there be ghosts haunting us as well?

I'm going to have to do some research ... In my spare time. Ha!

Who Am I to Judge? (K.t. and Friend)

"I get it. The addiction thing. I can easily see why people get sucked up into the drug scene. I loved doing heroin."

"Wow. I never knew you did that shit."

"Oh, yeah. Jason and I did all kinds of drugs. We had a blast. Laughed our asses off. So I understand why people get hooked. I'm just lucky. I must not have that addiction gene. I was able to say I'll do heroin five times and be done with it. And I *was* done. I'll never do it again."

"Thank God … That stuff is nasty. I've known so many young people who have died from it. It's so sad. I'm glad you were able to say you'd never do it again and follow through. I wish I could say 'I'll never do that again' about something as simple as smoking. I get so mad at myself for not being able to quit. I'm sure drug addicts beat themselves up, too. That's why I can't judge 'em when they struggle to quit but keep relapsing."

"Yeah, I can't judge anybody. Who am I to judge?"

"I feel the same way. Who am I to judge anyone about anything?"

You, my dear, are the most beautiful girl I've ever laid eyes on. You're funny, smart, and creative. You deserve to feel good-- be happy. I'm so sorry that I've let you down and let things go this far. I'm so sorry that I was so caught up in the craziness of our life that I was blinded to how you've been feeling and dealing with it all. I just want you to know I love you more than you could know.

As your mom, sometimes I have to make tough decisions. In this case it is getting you the help you need although you don't want it. I wasn't given a guide on how to be a good parent, but I'm going with my gut on this one. Enough is enough.

You have been feeling hopeless for way too long. It's not fair. There is a lot of sweet goodness in the world, a lot of beauty you can't see because you are hurting so much. I want to be able to at least give you hope. I'm sorry I can't do it on my own. I need help. That's why I've done some research and found a program that has been proven to be successful in helping people all over the world with their eating disorders. It's a program many adults wish they knew about when they were teens, so they could have intervened earlier to prevent the permanent damage done to them by the illness.

It's only natural that you want to resist. Especially when you think you're fine. But because you're "in it," you can't see what I see--a beautiful girl who is in need of help.

Since you've probably felt abandoned for so long, I'm sure you're going to wonder why now? I'm sure you're going to say I'm fine like you always do, and I'm sure you're even

(Continued)

going to hate me for interrupting your junior year, but this treatment program needs to happen.

I know you don't want to miss school. I know you're worried about what people will think. I know it must be totally overwhelming, but our first priority is for you to be healthy—mentally and physically—and it needs to happen now. Before more damage is done.

Being a teenager is hard enough without all of the crap you have been through. My heart aches for you. It's very painful for me to make you do something you don't agree with. But maybe someday you'll understand and be grateful that someone in your life cared enough to risk being hated to do something positive for you.

I can't crawl in your head and feel what you're feeling, and you are right—I don't understand what you're going through. But I do understand this program can help me help you.

As I said, I love you more than you could know. So does Dad. That's why we are both taking you to an assessment at the eating disorder clinic on Thursday. I'm letting you know now so you have time to wrap your head around it.

You are our beautiful flower, Lavender, and we don't want to see you wither away. We don't want to lose you.

Please try and understand and seek deep within and know you are worthy of feeling better.

Love and hugs and tickle-sniff-kisses,

Mom

<u>*I have my life back*</u>   *Friday, December 2*

My neighbor Abby shared this with me today: "This is the first time I've gotten out of bed and put real clothes on and actually put makeup on in months. I love my new bipolar medicine. It's awesome. I have my life back. I can't believe I feel this good."

I'm soooooo happy for her!

I pray my family can find relief with the right medicine . . . or with whatever it takes …

I'm Fine (K.t. and Lavender)

"I am *not* gonna be locked up to gain weight. I've already gained ten pounds and look fat. I used to be beautiful until you butted in to my business. I'm fine."

"You think? Is that why you passed out three times this week at school and once at home and had to go to the hospital for an EKG to check out your heart?"

"I don't care about my heart. I am *not* gonna be locked up in an institution. You saw how it affected your son when he was in the mental ward. It didn't make him better—it made him worse. You want me to get worse?"

"First of all, *it* didn't make him worse. *He* made himself worse by not following the doctor's advice. Second, I want you to get better. That's why I'm saying you need to get treatment. You're not going to be locked up. It's intensive out-patient, so you'll come and go."

"Why do you always care too late? You always wait until it's too late to do anything. Forget it. I'm fine now."

"I'm sorry I've been so consumed with your brother that I didn't know what was happening with you. He's so blatant with his mental issues and you're so sneaky. How am I supposed to know when you hide everything so well? I'm sorry I can't read your mind, but I am trying, and I do care. That's why I'm taking you to the mood disorder group four days a week, your counselor weekly, and the psychiatrist twice a month. And it's why I pushed for the 504 plan to change up your high stress class schedule. When you started losing your hair and passing out, I took you to an assessment at the eating disorder clinic, but you refused to do what they wanted. When you convinced me you could get better at home, I agreed to let you try it for a while, but I can't let it go on any longer. We made an agreement that if you weren't feeling better within a couple of weeks you'd agree to go. But you're refusing. Do you want to die?"

"Yes. Actually, yes. I hate my life. I just want to disappear. I want to go to sleep and never wake up."

I'm Fine (Continued)

"That's why I'm taking you to the clinic, Lavender. I love you so much and I can't stand watching you be so unhappy. You are worthy of living a happy life. I'm sure it's hard for you to see when you're in it, but you're not seeing things clearly because you're sick. You need professional help and I'm getting it for you. What else do you want me to do?"

"Nothing. I want nothing from you. I'm fine."

Wow. When I look back and see how I reacted to my daughter, I realize I was in the defense mode. Rather than listening to her and responding in a gentle, supportive way, I went on and on about what I was doing to help her. I, I, I. I made the entire conversation about me instead of her. I still don't know what the correct words would have been, but I see now why she wanted nothing from me. I can't even imagine how overwhelmed she must have felt.

I Pray

I pray
I dig deep enough
find real enough
heed soon enough
my Truth
that knows

. . .

and grow.

I pray
they dig deep enough
find real enough
heed soon enough
their Truth
that knows

. . .

and grow.

I pray
we all dig deep enough
find real enough
heed soon enough
our Truth
that knows us all
that knows the All
so we all

. . .

evolve.

Ghost lady found!   _Tuesday, January 10_

Today I learned about a "ghost" lady when meeting with one of my students about her journal writing. My student said the woman helped her family out a lot with the wackiness going on in their house and gave me her number. Leonard will probably think I'm dealing with the devil if I bring that woman into the house, but I'm going to talk to both of them and give it a shot. What do we have to lose?

*Already Tried That One**

20 mixed up, A to Z,
and many missing in between:
Abilify, Busbar, Zoloft, Lamictal,
Effexor, Prozac, Lithium, Risperdal,
Trazadone, Geodon, Xanax, Seroquel,
Remeron, Latuda, Tranqueline, Adderall,
Vyvance, Wellbutrin, Paxil, Zyprexa,
And this list here is only some of the All.

* The author is not denouncing any of these medicines.

Attitude on Addiction

How appropriate—
the rain ...
pouring,
pounding,
roaring like a train.
It's appropriate
for our grieving
and all its gloom
when we're
alone together or
alone
in separate rooms--
worn-down with worry
sadness and frustration,
confused when confronted
with our children's
situations,
but mostly distanced
by our attitude
on addiction

...

I'm Done (K.t. and Leo)

"I'm done. I can't take it anymore. I'm done with him coming home all fucked up and scaring the crap out of us. I'm done wrestling with him to stop him from jumping out the window to kill himself. I'm too old for this. I probably only have another ten years in me to continue creating, if that, and maybe only another twenty to live, if I'm lucky. I'm not gonna spend the rest of my life living like this. I'm done."

"He doesn't remember a thing. Although he was walking and talking, he was totally blacked out. That wasn't him who was wrestling with you. That was *not* our son. Why would he wrestle with the person he wants most in the world to be loved by? You can't take it so personally. He is stuck in the bottom of the abyss of the addiction cycle and can't get out. He needs help."

"He needs to get a job. Then he will be too busy to get fucked up."

"He needs to get sober and stay sober by getting the right mental health treatment. He will never be able to keep a job right now. He does all the drugs cuz he's anxiety-filled and depressed and—"

"He needs to suck it up. I deal with all of that, too--every single day--but I suck it up. He needs to suck it up, stay off the drugs, and get a fucking job."

"And how do you suppose he can get a job and keep it when he's homeless?"

"Well, that's his problem. I'm sick of his problem affecting me … and you. Look at what he's doing to you. Us. You should be writing and being creative and enjoying your retirement. But every day you are crying and consumed with worry. I should be going to tractor shows, riding my bike, and canoeing down the river, but every day I am busting my ass trying to catch up for time I've lost because of him. We should be going to the German Club, traveling, and having fun."

I'm Done (Continued)

"I know. You're right."

"Do you see what is happening? We can't even leave the house, because every time we do something bad happens. I'm done with such a brilliant guy acting like a loser. I told you before I'm shaking the loser tree. He can be a loser somewhere else. I'm done. And you should be, too. We've tried over and over letting him come back here to live—we've gone above and beyond trying to get him the help he needs. I don't know how much longer you can take it, but I'm done. I know you're his mother ... and I know it kills you to kick him out ... so if you really want him to come back here from the hospital because you think it's the best thing--for you and him--for all of us--then bring him home--but I'm at the point, and I'm just letting you know, where it's him or me. One of us has to go. Cuz I'm done."

Where's the booze?????!!!!!!!!!

A hat filled with problems   Wednesday, February 7

I recently heard this: When a bunch of people were standing around complaining about their problems, someone suggested they trade their problem with someone else. Thinking they had the worst problem, they thought it would be a piece of cake to deal with someone else's. So, they all wrote down their biggest issue, put it into a hat, and then were instructed to pick out someone else's. What they discovered was that they weren't satisfied until they traded enough times to get their own problem back. Interesting …

"Oh, I get it now. I know why you're having such a hard time letting him go."

"What is it?"

"What I'm getting is that you've shared multiple past lives with him—and in the last one he was crippled—in a wheelchair—totally dependent on you. You were his sister. You watched him kill himself."

"Whoa."

"Yeah. It all makes sense now—why you try so hard to save him."

"What do I do now?"

"If you don't want him to repeat the pattern--if you don't want him to kill himself again in this lifetime--you have to totally let him go. Break off all communication."

"I can't do that. I love him too much."

"Yes, you can."

"How?"

"Send him light. Send him love. That's the only way he has a fighting chance. If he keeps running back home to his Mamma, he's never going to be able to break free, face his fears, learn his lessons. You have to remember you have your journey and he has his. He has to figure it out for himself. You can't keep rescuing him. You're actually hurting him more than helping him by always being there for him. And you're hurting yourself."

"He's told me that a few times before—that my loving him so unconditionally actually hurts him. But I can't let him starve. I can't let him freeze to death. I can't let him totally go. I *can't*—"

"You *can* if you want to help him. You *can* if you want to save him from himself."

"Can you help me?"

"What's your worst fear about him?"

"That he'll die."

"Ok. Imagine him dead."

"Errrrr. I hate that image."

"Just give it a shot while I try something."

"Alright. Here goes."

. . .

"Whoa. How strange. A feeling of peace just wrapped me with warmth. What happened?"

"I harmonized your chakras with the thought of him gone in your mind. So living with the fear of him dying won't be so hard for you. It will be easier for you to let go and let God take over."

"Thank you."

"You're strong and you love him more than anybody else. You *can* let him go. Words help manifest. Say the words 'I can' over and over. Go on—say them."

"I can … I can … I can. I can. I can. I can."

"You can let him go because you love him. This is your lesson, too, ya know. Your ability to love him enough to let him go will help him be able to do the amazing things he's here to do. Life is all about lessons and love and you have such an amazing love for your son. So amazing that you *can* let him go."

"Wow … I still feel peaceful—for the first time in a long time. This was an amazing session. So deep."

"Definitely deep. And so beautiful. Much can be gained from having a strong enough love to let go. We can all learn from that one."

Filleted

Being	pulled—
yanked—	like a fish
on a hook is	what I feel,
except it's not my	mouth that is ripped.
It' s my heart. This	burning pain moves in
waves, starting at my	jawline and sinking down
into my stomach, slicing	my heart in half on the way.
My heart's filleted, vulnerable,	tender. I want to be with
you but can't let you pull me in	this time. You say you've
changed, but I've heard that one	before. Hundreds of times I
took your bait. So, naturally, you	hooked, yanked, and reeled
me in. You squeezed, skinned me	alive, filleted me quickly, and
then I fried. In your hot oil. I know	there's no malice on your
behalf. You're a good fisher	man and you're just doing
what you're good at do	ing. Knowing what you
want. Getting what you	need. To survive. But
now, even though I've	wizened up and no
longer take your bait,	I still feel the hot,
pain moving in waves,	filling up, sinking
into my soul, and I	wish we could be
the way I imagine	us to be—All of

us living happily together
a school of fish
swimming peacefully and
happily in cool, calm waters.

"Why didn't you tell me about Lavender? I thought best friends were supposed to be able to share their lives with each other. But you totally cut me off. Maybe I could have helped you guys, for Christ's sake. Damn it. Talk to me."

"I couldn't tell you. Because she was suicidal. And I didn't want anyone to know and make things worse."

"Well, ya know you can tell me anything and I won't tell anyone."

"Uh, yeah. That's why when I told you about Aries's 'incident' it was all over Facebook the next day."

"I didn't post anything ... Oh, my ... God ... My kids must have!"

"Why the hell would you tell your teenagers when I told you not to say anything?"

"Cuz I was trying to use Aries as an example of why they shouldn't use drugs."

"Whatever. After one of Lavender's teachers slipped and told one of her 'concerned' friends that she wouldn't be in school for eight weeks because she had to go to an eating disorder clinic, Lavender found out half of the school knew the next day. I still don't know why her teacher told a student. Anyway, that night on the way to the clinic she tried to jump out of the car while we were doing 65 mph—scared the crap out of me. She didn't want anyone to know, so I was respecting her wishes. That's why I didn't tell you. At that time, we hadn't even told our family, yet. Nobody knew back then. Except my boss. I had to tell him, so I could get medical time off work."

"Oh, my God. I'm sorry I was so mad. I was just so hurt that you weren't responding to me."

"I'm sorry I hurt you. I'm sorry I felt like I had to isolate myself so much. At the time, I thought that was the only way I could salvage any trust that Lavender had left in me.

"I totally understand what you're saying now. I love you guys so much, and I love Lavender like my own daughter. I just freaked when I didn't hear from you. Cuz I worry about you."

"I should have given you a quick call to assure you we were hanging in there. But at the time, I just didn't wanna burden you . . . or anyone. Secrets are hard to keep. They're like a heavy load needing to be dropped—hard for anyone to carry around. I thought it would be unfair, almost torturous, for me to drop such a load on you and then ask you to keep it a secret. It sounds corny, but I think of that Ben Franklin quote: 'Three may keep a secret if two of them are dead.' I just have to be strong and carry my own burdens. Everybody has them. For some reason my family's burdens are pretty heavy right now. I just have to be strong. God wouldn't give me more than I can carry, would He?"

"I don't know. It just doesn't seem fair. I hate feeling so helpless. I can't even imagine how you must feel."

"You couldn't have done anything to help anyways. Really. It was a family thing and you were working and busy with your own kids. I do understand that helpless feeling though. Fortunately, sharing with members in my N.A.M.I. support group is really helpful. I'm learning ways to cope with the chaos and helplessness. Working also helps. It keeps my mind distracted. Leo, well, he does the best he can. He feels so sad for Lavender though. But, *please*. Don't spend your time worrying about us. I know it's easier said than done, but really … just keep being you--I love you--and I'll do my best to keep you in the loop when I can."

"I love you, too. Thanks for your honesty."

"Same."

Ghost lady clears house of ghosts!   Tuesday, March 7

The Ghost lady came over today. She said there are many ways to clear a house of spirits. She said she liked using the Christian way mixed with a bit of Native American and wondered if that would be ok. Of course I said yes. First she took out a pendulum and put it over each of our heads to see if we had any "attachments." I had her do Lavender first. She was clear of attachments, so I told Lavender to go take a bike ride. Leo and I were clear, but Aries wasn't, so she lit some sage, waved the smoke around him with an eagle feather, and said a prayer. Then she checked again and said the spirit moved somewhere else. I told Aries to catch up with Lavender, because he looked a little nervous. Ghost Lady went through our entire house, burning sage, sprinkling holy water, and drawing the sign of the cross on mirrors and at the top of each doorway. She found a ghost attached to an old chair having a needle-pointed magnolia seat that we found at an antique store. Another one was attached to the vanity in the bathroom that we got from a garage sale. Also, there were a bunch in Aries's bedroom just "hanging out." Aries had told me that he thought things were messing with him in his room, but I didn't believe him … until Lavender started talking about seeing a guy standing beside her bed while she was trying to sleep. In any case, we opened all of the windows and doors. Ghost lady said a bunch of prayers and asked them to go to the light. She said they all left except the one attached to the vanity in the bathroom.

(Continued)

Ghost lady said the ghost in the bathroom wore a high-necked Victorian dress and was obsessed with brushing her hair and looking at herself in the mirror. When I asked her if the ghost could be the woman who died giving childbirth in Aries's room, she said she was more likely brought into the house with the vanity. She said the ghost wasn't hurting anything, but if I felt uncomfortable that she was living in my bathroom, I could keep encouraging her to go to the light. Ghost lady left me some holy water and told me where I could buy sage.

Leo said the house seemed more peaceful. The kids said they liked the smell of sage. I'm going to buy some tomorrow. I'm willing to do anything …

My Fender Laguna Is Gone

My Fender Laguna
is gone.
The best sounding,
easiest to play,
most beautiful guitar
in the entire world.
My favorite gift of all from you
is gone--
has been gone for years.

Years ago, when I ran to the house
from Camp Site #1
during a spontaneous
acoustic jam session
I lost my breath
when I picked up
my Fender guitar case in my office.

Because it was empty.

What the hell?
Where was my gift?
My favorite guitar? My friend?
Why wasn't my
Fender Laguna safe inside its case?

My Fender Laguna Is Gone (Continued)

I gasped, in shock.
I scanned the room,
searched my thoughts,
fervently hoping
that the guitar I loved so much
and did my best to keep protected
was in safe hands.

I searched my property,
queried friends and family,
called the cops
and the pawn shops.

But it was too late.
If only I had made time to play it earlier,
I would have discovered its absence sooner.

A pawn shop owner said
it had come and gone—
the serial number proved it.
It was pawned by a kid.
Sammy was his name.
He stole my guitar
and he never even played it.

My Fender Laguna Is Gone (Continued)

I called the cops again
who went to the pawn shop,
but no records are kept of who buys.
I filled out a police report,
pressed charges, and a
warrant was put out
for the culprit's arrest—Yes.

But he had left the state—
was on the run—but it didn't even matter,
because my Fender Laguna was gone.

I just couldn't tell you.
I couldn't.
I'm sorry.

I wanted to protect myself from your anger and
I wanted to save you from
the stabbing disappointment you'd have in your son
for associating with Sammy and inviting him to our house.
I knew you would point fingers and
would want to blame
and I couldn't blame you—you had the right,
but it would only cause more tension
and it wouldn't change anything.
It wouldn't get back my precious guitar.

My Fender Laguna Is Gone (Continued)

So, I stuffed my sadness and
I stopped playing guitar
altogether,
too fearful that you'd find out and
too guilty to indulge.

Well, recently, Sammy,
the thief, the addict,
called me.
He said he was finally sober,
after running, relapsing,
being in jail
and rehab for years.
He said he came back
home from California
because he was working diligently
on the twelve steps and
wanted to meet with me
wanted to apologize
wanted to set things right.

Although my chest squeezed my heart
until it hurt
and I wanted to punch him,
strangle him, kick him where it counts,
make him suffer like I did,
I agreed.

My Fender Laguna Is Gone (Continued)

I agreed to meet him
because I know forgiveness is key
to my health as well as his.
Yes, forgiveness is key.

We met in the cemetery.
He said he was sorry—so sorry.
And even if I could never forgive him
at least he wanted to try and see
if he could somehow make it up to me.

I said, "The only true way would be
to find *my* Fender--I miss it madly.
I miss its sound, its vintage beauty,
its easy-to-play friendly spirit, and
I'm tired of feeling turned inside out,
hiding its absence from my husband,
protecting Aries from being blamed."

Sammy admitted that
Aries played no part—that his only fault was
being too nice, too kind, too trusting—
and Sammy said he'd do his best to
find my Fender
to help stop my suffering.

Sammy didn't have any luck.
I assume they're too loved to sell.
I don't have much hope, but I can only pray
that it will show up some day.

My Fender Laguna Is Gone (Continued)

So, now you know.
Now you know about
my fear and worry of your reaction--
how for years my gut has been twisted in knots,
grappling with guilt and
my heart has heavily heaved with hurt.

Just know I'm sorry.

Also know I'm working on moving on.
Life is too short—quickly go the years—
so I'm challenging myself
to play guitar again
to heal my heart
to remove my fears.

Please know I'll never forget
until my very end
my precious gift from you –
my Fender Laguna friend.

<u>*What's a mom to do?*</u>   *Wednesday, May 9*

Today, Aries said he couldn't believe all the bad things he'd done and that he was a terrible person. I told him not to think of himself as a bad person--that his actions were bad, not him. He refused to believe me. Then he said the universe didn't want him to care about his hygiene because brushing his teeth made him physically ill and taking a shower made him insane from itching. I told him he had sensitive skin and we could find things that wouldn't make him sick or itchy and to not give up on taking care of himself. He said it doesn't even matter. That nothing matters so he shouldn't even bother.

My, God. What is a mom to do?

Steady Betty

My kids say I'm sane—the only sane one in the house.
But who's to say who's sane and who's not?
Really. Who's to say?

Steady. Steady Betty they call me.
Never dramatic or hyper or angry.
Just the same.
Queen of restraint.
Steady.
Predictable.
Dependable.
Boring.

My kids are looking for action.
Change.
Excitement.
Intensity.

How can I possibly give them that?

I calm myself by thinking,
"We are each part of a whole.
I'm Steady Betty.
For now that's my role."

He's One of Us (K.t. and a Psychic)

"He says he doesn't want to steal or do drugs, and I don't really think he does. When he does that crap, he's not himself—he's not the Aries we all know and love. He's a different person. It's like he's possessed or something. Do you think I'm crazy?"

"Absolutely not. You're *not* crazy. But you're right about him not being himself. It's not him behaving that crazy way. He's being controlled by some dark entities. He *is* possessed."

"Why him? Why would some dark entities want him?"

"Because he's one of us."

"What do you mean?"

"He's psychic. A healer. He knows about other dimensions and has so much to give. He understands how the ego and energy operate. He's open to the All of what IS. He's intuitive and clairvoyant and intensely passionate about teaching everyone about the metaphysical world. That's why they want him. They want to block him from doing all the good he's here to do. They want to stop him from enlightening others. He makes it easy for them because he's so vulnerable."

"Why is that?"

"Because he cares … and is trusting. He's so kind and accepting of everyone that I wouldn't be surprised if he invites the demons in. The problem is he doesn't protect himself when he's doing readings with the Tarot—he told me he doesn't need to worry about dark stuff messing with him. But he *does* need to worry if he doesn't take precautions. Another reason he's so vulnerable is because of all the drugs he does. All those drugs create holes in his energetic barriers and make it easy for the demons to get in. He's gotta stop *all* of the drugs."

"How can he stop doing drugs when the demons are manipulating him to do them from within?"

"He needs to build up his defense system--so they'll move out."

"How can he do that?"

He's One of Us (Continued))

"Pray a lot. He needs to ask to be filled, surrounded, and protected by white light, divine love. The demons hate that. They hate the light and its high frequency. They like to keep it on the down low."

"So there's hope?"

"Always. There's always hope with prayer. Always."

The phone rang. I was dreaming. A policeman said we needed to pick Aries up from a party where there was underage-drinking. I was relieved Aries didn't drink but found out later he had just bought LSD.

The phone rang. I was teaching. A middle school principal said I needed to pick up Aries. He jumped off of the second floor stairway banister and a teacher thought he was trying to kill himself.

The phone rang. I was driving. A security guard said I needed to pick up Aries from the store. He was caught stealing cough medicine and was delirious.

The phone rang. I was sitting in our woods by a campfire, trying to celebrate our 25th anniversary. A mom called and said the police were looking for Aries and her son.

The phone rang. I was writing lesson plans. The principal said Aries had to be picked up from his high school and couldn't come back until he had a mental health/drug assessment. He was hiding under a table in the library making strange noises.

The phone rang. I was putting laundry away. The mental hospital's nurse said Aries was out of control and wanted to know if we approved of putting him on medicine to calm him down. Leo said absolutely not. He'd rather his son be put into a rubber room so he could work his frustration out than be put on addictive, prescription drugs. I told her yes, because I promised Aries that if he went to the mental hospital he could be helped with his anxiety.

The phone rang. I was grading papers. A psychiatrist from the mental hospital said Aries's moods were "rapidly cycling" and wanted to know if that was his base line.

The phone rang. I was writing bills. The dual-diagnosis rehab center for teens said it would only cost $35,000 for thirty days of treatment. They suggested he would need six months' treatment. We took out a second mortgage so he could go for at least three months.

The phone rang. I was at a N.A.M.I. meeting. A friend of ours on the rescue squad said he was on the call that took Aries to the emergency room. Aries was paranoid and delusional and hiding in some bushes when they picked him up.

The phone rang. I was trying to sleep. A nurse from the hospital said Aries had just been placed into the step-down unit from intensive care. His racing heart finally calmed.

The phone rang. I was reading. Aries called from a rehab center and said he earned enough points to come home for a weekend visit. I said I wasn't going to pick him up as he requested, because being home would be too triggering and he'd only been sober for six weeks. He said he couldn't believe that I didn't have faith in him. He said he would find his own way home.

The phone rang. I was cooking. Aries said he borrowed his friend's car and hit a tree and got the car stuck in the snow. He was huffing duster when I arrived.

The phone rang. I was crying. It was an insurance company. They wanted us to pay for a destroyed mailbox, fence, and tree.

The phone rang. I was still trying to fall asleep at 2 a.m. An emergency room social worker said Aries had been sent there because he was found delusional in a bar, saying he was the bar owner. I told her he needs to go to the mental hospital and then directly to rehab. She said she would help.

The phone rang. I was writing out lesson plans at 4 a.m. The social worker from the ER said that Aries would be discharged at 10 a.m. to the psych ward of a nearby mental hospital.

The phone rang. I was driving home from work. The nurse from the mental hospital promised me she would get Aries the help he needed and he would go directly from the hospital to a treatment program.

The phone rang. I was walking. Aries gave me his pin number so I could visit him in the psych ward. He said he was ready for treatment. I talked to the staff, reminding them that he could not come home, because I couldn't keep him safe and he needed to go to a duel- diagnosis rehab center after being stabilized. We made the contacts and set everything up with the insurance company.

The phone rang. I was driving to visit Aries. The social worker from the hospital said he was being released, but the rehab facility didn't have an opening for three more days. So, I brought him home, praying for the best.

The phone rang. I was folding laundry. The rehab facility finally returned my call. They said they couldn't take Aries now because he was already stable and they only took people who needed to go through detox.

The phone rang. I was trying to celebrate our 30th anniversary at the campfire in our woods. Lavender said the police were in the driveway and put Aries in handcuffs and took him away for underage public intoxication.

The phone rang. I was raking leaves. Aries asked if he could have some money put on his commissary because he didn't have any deodorant, toothpaste, or shampoo in jail.

The phone rang. I was crying. The crisis team said they couldn't find Aries at the location I told them to go. Aries had called saying he was going to kill himself if he had to be homeless another day, so I called the crisis center to help because I was at a funeral three hours away.

The phone rang. I was pacing at 1:00 a.m. A police officer said Aries had been hit by a car while riding a bike on a four lane road and refused to go to the hospital.

The phone rang. I was curled in the fetal position. The insurance company called and said the owner of the car that hit Aries wanted money to fix the damages to his car.

The phone rang. I was in a meeting at work. A mental hospital psychiatrist who had taken care of Aries at least six times before finally called me back, saying I'd better be a stricter parent and get a grip on my son or I was going to lose him to an overdose.

The phone rang. I was buying groceries. It was my aunt saying Aries had come to her house and was out of his mind, talking a hundred miles an hour about stuff that happened ten years ago. She wanted to help him but was taking care of babies and afraid to let him in.

The phone rang. I was unloading groceries. A deputy sheriff said he had responded to the 911 call from a driver who had almost hit Aries because he was passed out in the road. The deputy said he arrested Aries for intoxication from a harmful inhalant, which is a felony.

The phone rang. I was doing dishes. Aries called from jail saying he would be out in a few days because he was there for carrying around a dead squirrel, which is only a misdemeanor.

The phone rang. I was cooking breakfast. Aries said he was in jail. Again. He had no idea why.

The phone rang. I was actually napping. Aries called from the rehab center and said four months was the trick and he was now well enough to come home, go back to college, and make us proud.

The phone rang. I was cleaning the bathroom. The deputy of a college said Aries was caught inhaling a harmful intoxicant in class and was expelled until he had a hearing.

The phone rang. I was reading essays in my classroom. Aries asked if I could pick him up. He crashed the car while huffing on the way to court and couldn't drive home. The one time I finally forced myself to let Aries handle his own situation made things worse: His father's car was totaled and Aries went into manic mode.

The phone rang. I was paying bills. A social worker from the state mental hospital said I should come to a hearing to determine if Aries was mentally ill.

The phone rang. I was pacing. The police said they found Aries swimming naked in the creek. It was the middle of winter. They took him to the emergency room. Aries told them he was "purging away evil."

The phone rang. I was watching a documentary on the homeless in America with Leo. The police told us they found Aries sleeping in a tunnel at the elementary school's playground and made him leave and wondered why we couldn't let him come home.

The phone rang. I was trying to sleep. Aries said that the guy who owned the house he was crashing at was playing music so loud that his organs hurt.

The phone rang. I didn't answer it. Aries left a message saying I was a terrible mother for not letting her son live at home.

The phone rang. I was washing dishes. Aries told me he needed money because he gave another homeless man all of the money I had given him to survive for a week.

The phone rang. I was just waking up. Aries, barely audible, asked if I could take him to community service, so he wouldn't have to go to jail again.

The phone rang. I was driving. Aries said he wanted to see me. When I met him behind the bowling alley, he had burns on his lips from huffing and burns on his shoulder from rolling through a fire. He was drunk and sweating profusely and talking a mile a minute, saying he met Jesus.

The phone rang. I was sick. Aries said he was freezing and wondered if I could pick him up and drop him off at the homeless shelter. When I found him, he was passed out on the ground in a parking lot with a can of inhalant in his hand. I threw the can as far as I could and loaded him into the car and headed to the hospital. He came to and pulled out another can from somewhere and huffed it until he passed out again. When he came to he grabbed the wheel and almost made us wreck because he wanted me to take him back to the place I threw out the other can of inhalant. When I refused, he jumped out of the car while I was doing 50 mph and ran across four lanes of traffic into some woods. I searched for hours before heading home and calling the police.

The phone *didn't* ring. The phone didn't *ring*. The phone *didn't ring* for days concerning Aries. And … then … I … was afraid … to *not* answer the phone.

Don't Should on Yourself

I could've and I should've but I didn't, damn it. I made Aries do it on his own. "I can't keep rescuing him," I said. "He has to figure it out alone." Well, ya see how that turned out, don't ya? Who really learned from all this? I know I did. I learned that if I *could've* taken off work and driven him to court like my gut wanted me to, *I should've*, despite the hassle of interrupting the flow going on in my classroom. Because then we'd still have a work car that saved gas and carried tools and rescued Leo's back from loading and unloading a truck and we'd still have a kid who had a chance to make amends with the man he most admired.

Now all we have is a pissed off dad, bitter that his life became ten times harder without his work vehicle, and a depressed, wrecked kid without a will to live.

Don't should on yourself is what I had to say over and over to myself after the fact. *Don't should on yourself. Don't should on yourself. Don't should on yourself.*

When vacillating
being pushed and pulled to and fro
not really knowing which way to go
simply being moved by emotions
I need to remember
a warm and fuzzy feeling
not a feeling from the past
dredging dark depression and anger
or from a fabricated future
weaving in worn-out worry and fear.

I need to remember
a warm and fuzzy feeling

. . .

of love.

Walking On Egg Shells

I hear the
Crack. Crackle. Crack.
even when tiptoeing …

I feel the
Crack. Crackle. Crack.
even when I'm standing still, holding my breath …

A million little slivers of white shells
Crack. Crackle. Crack.

The sharp blades,
slender and curved,
triangles, squares
and obtuse rectangles,
all with pointy angles,
all once part of a whole,
now separated,
fragmented, incomplete,
impossible to put back together--
all small stabs—
pricks of pain—
pierce me.

Will this feeling ever go away—
this feeling of walking on egg shells?

Self-Sabotage

I'm so sad. We had to kick Aries out again. He came home drunk. The night before he was supposed to start community college again. We told him what his options were. Stay in his room and sober up or leave and don't come back. He chose to jump out his window to meet some friends. He leapt right into the *other* world. The homeless world. He called me later and said alcohol is a truth serum and brings out who he really is and he truly believes we don't like who he is. He said he had subconscious thoughts that we didn't want him to stay because he wasn't worthy enough to stay. He didn't believe me when I said we wanted him to stay so he could be safe. So he could have a future. I said we love him but hate seeing him all fucked up and out of control. I reminded him that it's his actions, not him we don't like.

Lavender said she can't even be around him. She's mad at me for never giving strict enough consequences. I told her that I called his P.O. and he wasn't going to be able to come back home. She seemed relieved but so sad. She said she doesn't understand. I told her I learned in my N.A.M.I. meeting that it's typical for people to fall off the wagon right when things are going to be great because they feel too much pressure to succeed. When we thought back, we remembered Aries having a breakdown/relapse right after winning the election for class president, before getting his license, after getting his job, and almost every Christmas, Thanksgiving, and Easter. Something usually happened and he missed out on great gatherings or opportunities. Lavender could list her own as well, so I guess it is true.

The next day Aries came back home. I didn't invite him in. I gave him numbers to various agencies, his medicine, socks, a hoodie, a t-shirt, granola bars, peanut butter, bread, and water. It was fricking 90 degrees and the mosquitoes were eating him up, so I put some repellent in his book bag, too. I told him this was the hardest thing I have ever done and am so sorry I enabled so long and he said it's not my fault and was concerned how he would get help with nobody to help him. I reminded him of the piece of paper having all of the agencies on it. I cried, but I felt a streak of strength ... and hope ... somehow.

Self-Sabotage (Continued)

Aries called me three days later. He said he was now living with people who did heroin. He said he understood why I always enabled him, because he kept trying to save them. He said he wished he had more energy in order to vibrate at a higher frequency so he could heal at the cellular level. I said I'd pray for that to happen. He said not to worry because everything is just as it is supposed to be. I said I'd do my best. He said he appreciated things more because he had no cushion like he did when living at home. He said it was good for him to be in survival mode because he would have to work hard to survive and even harder to succeed. He said he loved me and was sorry for everything. I said I loved him, too.

I hung up the phone and cried for an hour.

God help him. God help me.

I Don't Have Time

Leo burst through the door at midnight. I knew right away from the crazy look in his eyes that he worked all day and night without taking time out to eat. Rampaging through the refrigerator, yelling "Food! Food!" he didn't see the usual already-made-up plate, so he stuffed some lunch meat into his mouth and went to bed.

While making breakfast the next morning I said, "You need to stop and take time out to eat."

"When I'm working, I don't have time to stop and eat."

"Honey, you have to make time to eat."

"Like I said, I don't have time. I have a lot to do and no help. They have pills for everything these days, so why isn't there a pill to pop to give me sustenance? Although I don't do pills, I'd do that."

"That's ridiculous. A grown man has to eat. Were you at least able to sleep last night?"

"Not really. I had that dream again. I'm a soldier. I can't move because my legs are gone. I can't divert my eyes from staring into a man's face. He has no nose. He keeps whimpering, 'We're too young to die.' That's when everything goes white and I wake up."

"My, God. That's horrifying. What a nightmare."

"It's no big deal. I've had it hundreds of times. I only wish I could see the uniforms and guns to know what war it was."

"Yeah. Then you could critique it and make sure everything is historically accurate like you do when watching the history channel."

"Right on."

"Well, here's your breakfast, and there's a lunch in your cooler."

"Thanks," he said, grabbing a piece of bacon off his plate and running out the door.

"Hey," I yelled. "Come back and get your cooler."

"I don't have time."

I stare at his uneaten breakfast, wondering. Could the dream be his recall of a past life obviously cut short? Could that be why he works like a madman and feels so anxious and rushed in this lifetime?

I'm Done (Song Lyrics)

How did it get this way? You ask.
How'd we let things go this far?
How'd we let things slip away? You wonder.
How come we're so at war?

I'll tell ya … I rob Peter every month to pay Paul.
I have three jobs you have none at all.
After moving in you stuck me with bills—
turned your head away high on your thrills.
Last night you said that you'd love me forever.
Tonight you slept with my best friend, Heather.
You're so capricious, I can't believe
a single word any day of the week.

How did it get this way? You ask.
How'd we let things go this far?
How'd we let things slip away? You wonder.
How come we're so at war?

I'll tell ya … I got sucked up in your fucked up routine.
Black and white just isn't my scene.
At least ya taught me to say what I feel—
at the moment make it real.

Right or wrong say what's on your mind, you said.
Let 'er rip, totally unwind.
Well, I'm tired of the crazy ride—
not gonna let my feelings hide, cuz I'm done.
I'm through with you.

How did it get this way? I ask. How'd I let things go this far?
Why'd I lose myself in you? I wonder.
How come I even fought this war?
Well, I'm done … I'm through … with you.
I'm done, done, done, I've had it with you—
I'm done. I'm through with you.

I got more out of AA meetings than Aries ever did. When he was forced by the courts to go and I took him, I was rapt by the stories and inspired by the strength of will that people had to help them make healthy changes.

Aries, however, said he didn't like sitting around listening to other people's problems, and he said hearing their success stories felt like a slap in his face. My cousin Johnny feels the same way as Aries. When I asked Johnny about the intensive out-patient treatment program and AA meetings mandated by the court for his third DUI, he said they were all bull shit and a waste of his time. He said everybody was really nice to him though because he told some funny stories and picked them up and dropped them off for meetings. He said he still drinks every day after meetings so he can relax before going to bed, so he's obviously not ready to quit. Maybe he'll never be.

As for Aries, he went from doing drugs to drinking, which everyone says is better, but I don't know. Aries says he needs to drink to keep his sanity, and I see how happy he is when he's drunk. But after the fact, alcohol makes him sick. He misses a lot of goodness happening around him. I get so sad because he reminds me of Dad and Johnny. I don't think I can stand watching another torturous demise of someone I love.

Maybe it's time for me to check out Al-Anon.

The Addict's Back

Leo and I decided to give Aries another chance to live at home. He had been in jail for 58 days and had gone through the jail's treatment program. Plus, it was only 0 degrees outside—the coldest winter we'd had in a long, long time. When Aries asked if he could go for a walk and I said yes, Lavender got mad at me and said I wasn't being a good parent and she didn't want to have to be one. She said Aries shouldn't be able to leave the house and should be treated like a dog. Later I understood why she felt that way. He put her through hell, I guess, way more than I realized at the time. But, after being in jail for so long and gaining 40 pounds, he needed some exercise. I thought I should let him go for a walk. Well, I was wrong, and I'm walking on egg shells. Again.

When the addict, the big, pink elephant that changes everything, is back in the house, I seek the light—imagine everything is going to be alright, live in a fantasy world that things will be different this time. But reality confronts me sooner than I expect:

Ahhhhhhhhhhhhhh …

In the morning, Leo sees the can of duster in the garbage. He goes to Aries's room to tell him he has until Monday to leave and stomps down the stairs. I hear a satanic voice coming from the bedroom. I walk in and see the trembling, sweaty body, the contorted face. Aries has another can of inhalant and won't let me take it from him—does it right in front of me—so I tell him he has to leave right away. He says he's gonna kill himself, so I call 911 and the whole thing starts again. He takes the phone from me while I'm talking to 911 and says things are fine and his mom is just over-protective. He leaves and the cops find him down the road. They pick him up and bring him home. They want to know if I want them to pink slip him—force him to be hospitalized without his consent. I think *Why don't they arrest him?* but I say the ER will just let him go because Aries can talk his way out of anything. I call the crisis team. They talk to the police officer who is still in the cruiser with Aries.

The Addict's Back (Continued)

The crisis counselor says I'm right—that Aries will talk the ER social worker into thinking he is ok—not suicidal and/or homicidal, because he is totally lucid, speaking intelligently and articulately. It's the nature of the drug—it makes people crazy one minute and clear-headed the next. The counselor says he's going to check on something and calls back in a few minutes. He called an out-of-our county homeless shelter which has two nights available. The police officer takes him to the shelter.

At 11 p.m., the shelter calls me and says Aries is too much of a liability because he admitted to the in-take person that he has not taken his psych meds for over a month because they wouldn't give them to him in jail. The shelter says Aries admitted that he didn't care because he's tired of being a drone and wants to live without the meds—enjoy the mania and then deal with the depression rather than feel nothing. The shelter says Aries tells them he can't remember the last time he used any drugs. Does he really not remember?

I speak to Aries and he says he's gonna start hitch-hiking and since he doesn't have a phone or know where he is, he says this will probably be the last time I ever hear from him. He says he loves me and is sorry for everything.

I go outside into the 10 degree night, get into my car, and start driving to the shelter. The wiper blades can't keep up with the snow on the windshield. And I can't stop crying.

Pooped-on-deeode by Karma (K.t. and Aries Driving Home from the Homeless Shelter)

"I really don't know if I can do this anymore, Mom. I just wanna die. The only reason I'm holding out is because I don't wanna do that to you, Dad, and Lavender."

"You might not feel that way if you got the right help. You might have another 80 amazing years in front of you."

"Why would I wanna live another 80 years without my drugs of choice … or on prescriptions that make me feel like a zombie?"

"Well, maybe you've forgotten how good life can be without your drugs of choice. It might not be as bad as you think. You've been doing drugs a third of your life. Maybe you'll find that life is really worth living sober and maybe you'll get on the right meds to help your chemical imbalance."

"But people are so judgmental and don't get me. And now that you called the cops I'm fucked. My P.O. will never drop the felony this time. He already told me that the next time I got caught it would be seven months' jail time. He's been so lenient … but he won't be this time. So I will never be able to get a teaching job with a felony. I'll never be able to be a professor. I'm screwed. I'll never be the same if I go to jail for that long. Corey changed when he was put away for that long. And he's never been the same."

"Well, maybe Corey's a better man for it. He's not in jail and he's not doing drugs that are melting his brain."

"But he's not Corey anymore. I would rather be who I am and die than live not being who I am."

"You're more than a drug addict, Aries. Maybe you could plead for treatment instead of seven months' jail time."

"I know. I need treatment. But my P.O. already told me I need punishment, not treatment, because I already had the 30 day jail treatment, so he thinks I should be fine now. He said I need to be punished because I am a criminal. Am I a criminal because I huff compressed air? Why did you have to call the cops? It was a family thing."

"Well, I didn't call the cops because you were huffing. I called them because you said you were gonna kill yourself. Dad gave you the chance to stay 'til Monday after he told you he found the can. Then you had to go and huff more in your room after he said that. And then you did it right in front of me and wouldn't give me the can and you scared the crap out of me when you were shaking and sweating and talking like some kind of demon. So I made you leave right then. You made a promise that you wouldn't do drugs at home. So what was I supposed to do?"

"Well, if I were a parent and my kid was doing drugs, I would put him in a cage and hide the key until he regained his sanity. I made it for two months without huffing, so you could've said, 'Hey, you made it for two months this time so you have to extend the time before you do it again or you're out.' But you just threw me out."

"Well, I didn't just throw you out. I called the crisis team who made arrangements for you to get into the homeless shelter."

"Yeah, and you see how well that played out, don't you? They wouldn't keep me because I was honest with them and said I stopped taking my psych meds, so they said I had to go. And here you are picking me up at 1 a.m. two hours away from home. I'm just a fucked-up loser. And I have nothing to live for. I have no phone, no job, no car, no girlfriend, and again, no home. I'm not blaming you, Mom. You're an angel. I love you and I don't want you to ever think any of this is your fault. But I just don't want to live any more. I suck at living in this third dimension. It's not worth staying here to learn whatever lesson I'm here to learn. I'm a loser at life. I don't know how to take care of myself and I'm never gonna get better. I don't know how to be an adult. I just wanna die. I'm sorry, Mom. I'm really, really sorry."

"Well, we're going to go to the hospital right now."

"No. We're not. What are they gonna do there? Lock me up and make me crazier than I already am? Force me to take meds that don't help? Treat me like I'm an animal?"

"Your experience hasn't always been like that and you know it. There have been some really nice people who've helped you get back on track. Many times. I'll help you get into another program. We can work through this. Things *can* get better."

"Yeah, but it's just so hard to stay on track, especially when I'm homeless. I need to *feel* something, but I feel nothing. Nothing excites me or surprises me anymore. Everything is so boring. I have nothing to live for. I'd rather die."

"That's why I'm taking you to the hospital. I am *not* gonna let you kill yourself. You are too special. You have too much to give. The world needs you. I want you in my life. I have faith in you. I want you to have faith in you, too, and believe that things will get better."

"Mom, I can kill myself anywhere—all I have to do is a Jiu-Jitsu move and I'm done. So putting me in the hospital is only going to cost a lot of money and be a waste of time and it's not going to save me from myself. "

"What is?"

"Me. I am the only one who can save me from myself. The hospital won't keep me anyways because I'm no longer psychotic, I'm not homicidal, and I'm not suicidal anymore."

"But you …"

"Really … Honest. I'm not suicidal anymore. I'm sorry I said any of that out loud. I'm just venting. I need to get out the energy or it builds and then I wanna rage. Unfortunately, you're the only one around to hear me. But you're right. I have to have faith that things are gonna be okay. Please drop me off at Donny's. We'll watch some movies and I'll talk to you tomorrow. I promise."

"So you can truly promise me you're not gonna kill yourself tonight? I can leave you and not live the rest of my life in regret because I didn't take you to the hospital?"

"Yes. I promise. Even though I've fucked up my life again and been pooped-on-deeode by karma, I know I gotta deal with it. It might as well be in this lifetime."

"I'm glad to hear you're willing to deal with your life. I have faith in you. And I have faith that you're not just bullshitting me."

"I'm not."

"OK, then. I have to have faith. Be good to yourself, and call me when you wake up tomorrow. I love you."

"I will, and love you too, Mom. I love you, too."

I'm not done   _Nami meeting   Tuesday, October 10_

Meeting highlights:

_-- Don't say "I'm done" or "I can't" because that's not true …
I guess I better revise my "I'm Done" song!_

_-- You have a life. They have a life. We all need to live our own
life … Easier said than done._

_-- You don't want to be 70 years old and still tending … Every
meeting I hear this withered up woman talk about how she's so
tired of taking care of her adult children in their 50's. I do not
want to be like her. The group leader advised the woman to
read Melody Beattie's <u>Codependent No More</u>. I think I'll check it
out as well._

_-- You might be scared but you can handle a lot … I don't give
myself enough credit for what I do._

_--Focus on the what, not the how … I have to have faith that the
laws of the universe will allow the how to happen if I keep
focusing on the what. I need to practice this type of thinking
more. In fact, I need to put all of the laws of attraction into
action._

Ghost Lady Phone Call

"Hello."

"Hello, there. I am just checking in," said the Ghost Lady.

"Oh, that's nice." I paused, thinking about my morning with Lavender.

"I was driven, actually, to call you today. I hope you don't mind," she continued.

"No, I don't mind," I said. "I'm glad you did because I was actually going to call you."

"How are you children doing?"

"Actually, not so well."

"I had a feeling something's been going on. I don't mean to alarm you, but I've been feeling a lot of dark energy coming from your house when I drive by, and I was hoping I could come to the house again soon and help you take care of that."

"Yes. Please do. Aries had a major relapse while in his bedroom. And Lavender told the doctor last week that when she woke up from a nightmare there was a man by her bed and she tried to kick him. Then, this morning I ran into her room because she was screaming. She said she had just seen the man at the end of her bed again and wondered if I had seen him, too. Do you think this man is a ghost or just part of her dream?"

"Unfortunately, I'm pretty sure it's a ghost, and I think we should get rid of it before it becomes too attached to either Aries or Lavender. Does Lavender like to paint?"

I thought that question odd at this point in the conversation, but I said, "She's very artistic." I didn't mentioned to her that Lavender had asked a couple of weeks ago if she could remove the wallpaper in her room and paint the walls a different color.

"Perfect. Because I wanted to tell you I think she needs to reclaim her room, and the way she needs to do that is to repaint it and move things around. Aries should do the same. Ghosts hate that stuff. It may help them leave."

Ghost Lady Phone Call (Continued)

Coincidence? Hmmm. In any case, Ghost Lady said after I boxed up Aries's belongings and Lavender changed her room to her liking that we would do a cleansing and ask the angels to help us lead the spirits out of our house and to the next level where they need to be. So, Lavender is up painting her room with Leonard, and I'm taking all of Aries's stuff to the attic. I'll have Ghost Lady come and do the cleansing with the burning sage and holy water and prayers when Lavender isn't around. The thought of a true ghost in the house scares the bajeebees out of her. At this point, if it *is* ghosts causing any of this, I'll be more pissed than scared.

<u>Drunk People</u>   *Thursday, December 20*

*I love getting together with friends and family for the holidays,
but I can't stand being around drunk people who keep
repeating themselves over and over
and keep talking louder and louder about*

nothing.

! Means Yes

You stay strong. Stop enabling.
Separate yourself.
Walk away.

Shame devastates.
They apologize.
They hate themselves for causing pain.

You go back. You love them.
Your heart is lighter when they're lucid.
You gain hope. Too soon.
A trigger flips them.

You stare in disbelief and ask,
"How could you?
Why would you do it again
with everything to lose?"

You stare in the mirror, thinking,
"Why do you
choose to relive this hell again?"

Are you both possessed?
Have no control?
Hate yourselves?
Filling a hole?

Do they have a choice?
?

Do you?
!

The ghost lady told me when clearing my house of spirits by myself that I should consider the following:

1. *Keep the Bible open.*
2. *Ask God to give me guidance for what passages from the Bible to read.*
3. *Ask for my spirit guides and guardian angels to protect and guide me.*
4. *Pray while walking through the house counter-clockwise while burning sage.*
5. *Make crosses using holy water on windows, door entrances, and mirrors.*
6. *Open all of the doors and ask whatever is "not of light" to leave.*
7. *Praise and give thanks that lost spirits find the light.*

Looking forward to the right timing …

September 22

Dear Chief:

Thank you for helping out our son by suggesting the mental health court. I told Aries he should heed your guidance so he can have his life back. Initially, he said he'd do whatever was the quickest way out, but I think it is sinking in that it may take some serious time to make things right. Although a two year commitment with the mental health court seems overwhelming, I told him that he won't be able to come home until he completes a program and that going through a program that offers him so many opportunities is better than staying in jail.

He has been wanting to do his college assignments while he is in jail, but he doesn't realize that he is suspended until he has his hearing there. I spoke with the college psychologist and he is postponing the hearing until things are more settled.

I have been collecting dates of hospital stays, out-patient programs, psychiatrist visits, and all prescriptions he has been on. I need to give all of this information to the mental health court judge, so he can get into the program and out of jail as soon as possible.

Leonard and I appreciate your help and feel blessed that you, the Chief of Police, have taken so much of your personal time to visit Aries in jail and to help us with Aries over the years.

Keep smiling and God bless,

Katarina and Leonard Wilde

We Have a Choice

We meet expectations
because promises were made
or we don't.

We compromise,
rearrange, make space
because of change
or we don't.

When it all comes down to it,
we make choices
that we simply put up with
wildly embrace
resist
fight against
or ignore.

Any choice can
debilitate
or make
us stronger.

We have a choice.

Cognizance (Song Lyrics)

We can't change our lives
over someone else's destiny.
We can just send love their way and pray.

People have made commitments molecularly.
They or we can't see them … scientifically.

As much as we want to save them,
oh, so badly,
their old patterns may take them, so naturally.
Their old patterns will seize them, so easily.

As we stand and watch with tears,
their fears bring destruction.

With cognizance they create their fate.
With cognizance they create their fate.
With cognizance they create their fate.

Repeat song instrumentally.

As we stand and watch with tears,
our fears bring destruction.

With cognizance we create our fate.
With cognizance we create our fate.
With cognizance we create our fate.

Brave and evolved souls   Saturday, March 4th

I was intrigued today at the spirit guide workshop when the instructor said, "The most brave and evolved souls choose the most difficult challenges to experience on Earth." It gave me something to ponder: Do people purposely choose hardships for the sake of their personal evolution? If so, I'm even more inspired by so many who march forth with their heads held high, despite the serious issues they face daily.

Yeah! I Love this date!

Dear Doctor S.   April 22

I faxed two items: the letter from the courts for jury duty and information for food assistance. Aries didn't give the papers to you when you visited him on Saturday because he said he was "in the zone" and never wants to impose. He appreciated so much that you actually came to meet him where he is staying, and so do I.

If you feel comfortable writing a letter stating he has a mental condition that renders him incapable of jury duty that would be very helpful. I can't believe the courts are making me get a doctor's letter to get him out of jury duty even after I explained that he was homeless. Even if he were in a better state, Aries told me he would be too paranoid about going into a courtroom and could never handle the emotional stress of determining another's fate.

Also, I talked to his case manager and she said a letter could help him get food assistance. He had it for two months after getting out of jail because he was homeless but needs to re-apply and have a doctor's note stating that he is incapable of working at this time.

His case manager and I helped him fill out social security disability paperwork, but since he didn't have enough work hours he was denied. Now we have to work on supplemental security income (SSI). As you know, meeting up with him to take care of details is hit and miss, but we do our best. He does now have Medicaid, and I chose a carrier that you and his family doctor will accept.

The letter for jury duty must be given to the courts by this Wednesday. Thanks so much for your time and for caring so much about my son.

Sincerely,

Katarina Wilde

Disability Remarks for SSI Form

I had my dear friend who's a therapist help me write the following letter needed for the disability section on the SSI form for Aries. It freaked me out to read again, because I'm still having qualms. What if Aries got the right treatment and could work? What if he blows money on drugs if he does get assistance? My friend assured me he needs it and everything will work out. This is what we wrote:

As Aries's mother, I am heart-broken that my son's severe and persistent mental illness has debilitated him to the point where he can't work. He has been homeless since he was eighteen. He has slept behind dumpsters, lived on the streets, stayed in homeless shelters, and couch surfed. He has been hospitalized 16 times, all before he was twenty-one years old.

Often filled with anxiety that makes him physically ill, he is overwhelmed by even simple tasks such as grocery shopping or washing dishes. It is very difficult for him to attend/participate productively in mental health appointments because of his mood swings.

During times of his depression, he can't get out of bed, believes he is worthless, and has suicidal thoughts. When he has energy, he makes all kinds of grandiose plans like taking karate lessons, filling out job applications, visiting his grandmother, going back to college, and becoming a doctor of psychology. However, a day or hour later he can't even consider his plans because his mood shifts and he can no longer tolerate being in public or even thinking about previous plans.

Also, at times he is delusional. He believes he can manifest material things. For example, he told me how a car manifested at one house when he left it at another and how a shirt in his dresser manifested in front of his eyes so he could wear it. He also at times believes he is a ninja.

His illness prevents him from having insight into the seriousness of his condition. Because he is living in such unstable places, his anxiety and disorganized thinking makes his illness even worse. Having a stable environment could help him tremendously.

Please help my son by expediting a hearing for his disability. He is a kind and gentle soul and has a lot to offer the world.

Sincerely,

Katarina Wilde

I Don't Know Why I Do What I Do (K.t. and Aries)

"What's gonna happen to me when I get outta this mental hospital? Where am I gonna go? Where am I gonna live? Am I still gonna be a part of the mental health court?"

"I don't know."

"Can't I just come home? Please, can't I just come home?"

"No. You can't. I'm sorry. I had faith that I could let you come home for a few days and get re-grouped after being in jail—I felt so bad for you—but just like so many times before—you bit the hands that fed you. I don't know how to help you—I've failed over and over to help you. And you have no idea of how you are affecting us because you're there but not *there* when things happen."

"What happened?"

"You came home all fucked up and tried to take Lavender's medicine. When I tried to take the bottle away from you, you started wrestling me for it which pissed off Dad. Then you two got into it and you freaked out and said you wanted to kill yourself and kept trying to jump out the window and kept beating your head against the bed board and twisting your neck and making yourself pass out. It was terrible. The cop had to use the stun gun on you three times when you were wrestling with Dad before you went down. It was so, so sad and painful to watch. Lavender and I were horrified."

"Well, subconsciously I must really be in a lot of pain if I was trying to kill myself."

"I'm sure you are. This must be so hard for you. My heart aches for you."

"You think your heart is hurting. Well, mine is more than you could ever imagine. I don't even know why I did all of those drugs. I don't even like them. I can't believe I fucked up. I can't believe I fucked up again. Now I'm homeless … again. Damn it. I can't be homeless again. I can't be homeless again, Mom. I can't do this anymore."

"Will you be willing to try a program?"

"I can try, Mom. But I can't make any promises."

"Well, at least you're being honest. Before you used to promise and I believed you. You always sounded so sincere."

"I was always sincere when I said stuff, Mom. Why would I want to lose my opportunity to live at home, work at the music store--the perfect job for me--and go to college? Why would I want to lose everything and everyone I love? What's wrong with me? All I want is to live at home, get a job, and go to college."

"It's like you sabotage yourself every time you have an opportunity to better your life. You did it before running for class president, before getting your license, after getting a job, after getting into college."

"Maybe subconsciously I don't think I deserve a chance because of all the heartache I've caused—maybe I'm getting pooped on because karma is kicking my ass. I don't know why I fucked up again, Mom. I'm just a fucked-up loser and I don't know why I do what I do."

Biting the Hands that Feed (K.t. and a Friend)

"Aries *needs* to live with you. You have to let him live with you. Why won't you let him?"

"I tried. Believe me, I did. I tried to let him live with me. But he bit the hands that fed him. Over and over. I walked on egg shells every day. I couldn't breathe. I couldn't sleep. I tried to rescue him in every way. It just wasn't healthy."

"But he swears he won't do any more drugs and he swears he's gonna take his medicine. I believe him, and I think you should, too. He's the smartest person I know. He's the nicest person I know. You have to help save him. You have to let him come live with you. You just have to."

"I truly believe he means it when he says, 'I promise it won't happen again. I promise I won't do any more drugs. I promise I will take my medicine and help around the house. I promise.' I swear he means it when he says it. He convinces me and himself and everyone. And I know he doesn't have a fighting chance living on the streets—it's pretty brutal out there—so I let him come home, because he is so sincere, and because I believe he's right when he says he can never get better living on the streets. But year after year and tear after tear have come and gone and each false start left me with a hollow heart. I have to draw the line somewhere."

"But can't you do it one more time? Give him once more chance? I can't believe you--his own mother--doesn't seem to care. No wonder he's out of his mind. I can't stand seeing him like he is right now--so lost and hopeless."

"It's not that I don't care. I care more than anyone can imagine. It's just that my hands have been bitten off. So don't tell me I *have* to let him come home. Before you tell me what I *have* to do, *you* try taking him home and getting your fingers bitten off one by one and experiencing how lost and helpless *you* feel—how lost and helpless and sad and frustrated and worried and …"

"I'm so sorry. You're all such good people. It's just not fair. I'm so sad and so sorry—for all of you."

"Believe me, so am I. More than you will ever know. It's a shame that it can happen to the best of 'em."

"It's a damn shame."

122

Jail Visit

I went to see Aries in jail. He was sentenced to two weeks by the mental health judge for falling asleep during the meeting with his case manager. The judge told Aries he has never had a person fall asleep at a meeting established to help him. The judge said he was worried he wasn't taking his medicine, concerned about the bruises and burns on his face, and didn't like that he was living in a tent. I found it hard to believe that the judge of a mental health court didn't get to the root reason why he fell asleep during the meeting. Aries was/is in survival mode. His days and nights are mixed up because he wants to sleep during the day when he feels safer in public, and then in the evening, be one with the night, a ninja on guard. Aries told the judge he was taking his medicine, the bruises and burns were caused by learning new Ninja moves, and he was no longer living in a tent. He said he upgraded and was living in a man's house now. He didn't tell the judge that he could live there as long as he walked the ten mile trek to the store anytime he was told to get more alcohol by the house's owner who had a suspended license because of his DUI's.

In any case, he's on the 8th floor in jail—the psych ward—and seems calmer than when in jail before. He said he does ok until the pedophile pours his heart out to him and makes him feel sick. Or when he's crazy hungry. Being involved with the mental health court allows him to be on his medicine while in jail, but the prescription gives him a voracious appetite and makes him extremely tired so sometimes he misses meals because he sleeps right through them.

Aries read aloud a letter to me that he wrote and planned to give to the judge. In it he actually thanked the judge for putting him in jail, for giving him time to think about what his character flaws are, and for helping him figure out how to deal with them. He said he wants to be a humble man, an admired man, a man who shows his intelligence. He said he wants to be a man like the judge. The letter made me cry. It was so real, so honest. Aries really is a good guy. He says he really wants to get into the half-way house now. I pray he does.

123

Jail Visit (Continued)

Court day experience after two weeks in jail:

Well, the judge loved his letter, saying how Aries's vocabulary was perfect and message heart-felt. But the judge ordered him to go to jail again, this time for a week, for swearing at the people who had interviewed him while he was in jail to get into the half-way house. Previously, the judge let him slide for being cocky to the jail psychiatrist, testing positively for THC, and for missing his case manager appointment. I guess he had enough. Aries looked so sad when he left the court room with the police escort back to jail. I wrote him a letter and said I hope he can choose the right path to help him reach his goals. The problem is he keeps burning every bridge leading to his aid.

Hypocrite?

I do want to be healthy,
and I don't want to be a hypocrite,
so I say, "I have to quit smoking cigarettes,"
and I quit. I quit. I quit.
I've quit a hundred times.
So, how can I possibly say to him,
"Hey, you have to quit doing drugs,"
when I understand the challenge he faces,
the pull, the test, the struggle?
Who am I to say, "You're killing yourself.
Don't you want to live?"
when I'm coughing in the morning
and then lighting up again?
Who am I to say, "You're hurting others! Don't you care?"
when my second-hand smoke affects people everywhere?
I say, "I feel so guilty smoking—I'm such a hypocrite!"
So, how can I judge an addict,
knowing it's hard to quit?
People say, "Come on, it's different—
they certainly don't compare.
You're only smoking cigarettes.
He's doing dangerous drugs out there."
Whatever … I still battle against smoking,
and I beat myself up.
But, I do accept the facts:
I love to smoke; he loves his drugs.
No matter what consequences we face,
I've come to understand:
People will choose to do what they want—
and do what they can—'til they can't.

Is a Person Mentally Ill If ... ?

I received a letter from the probate court stating that an affidavit alleging Aries to be mentally ill subject to hospitalization by court order was filed. When I spoke with Aries's case manager for advice concerning advocating for or against this, her response was that it could help him receive more services if he were determined to be mentally ill. But the lawyer at the hospital told me he would never be able to shake that kind of thing from his record and would never be able to get a job; needless to say I was confused. How can these lawyers who don't even know my son determine if he is mentally ill? How can I trust the doctors at the various hospitals when they disagree on his diagnosis? Who am I to determine if he is mentally ill and that his psychosis is not due to all of the drugs he does? Is a drug addict mentally ill? Can anyone give an accurate diagnosis? Who knows? Well, I made a list of questions:

Is a person mentally ill if

1. he has a deep understanding of metaphysics and wrote a paper in high school about the string theory before it was explained on TV?

2. he creates and calls upon different personas (in my son's case, Rezlop and Dr. Pro) to help him deal with life's darkness, challenges, etc.?

3. he experiments on himself with prescription as well as street drugs to learn the effects on his thinking and behavior?

4. he rhymes all of his statements with the long "E" sound and asks me to bring him the frequency of "E" because that would help him heal while he is in the psych ward?

5. he does back flips off the second floor banister inside his school and off the roof outside of his school because someone dares him and he thinks it would be fun?

6. he is cognizant of how energy, ego, karma, and the laws of attraction affect individuals?

7. he abuses his own prescription medication so he can feel fabulous for a couple weeks of the month, producing insightful writing and music to accompany it, despite knowing that for the other two weeks of the month he will have no energy to do daily chores which causes arguments between him and his dad?

8. he believes he has seen things manifest in front of his eyes, including Jesus, and tells stories to prove each situation?

9. he views the world through various lenses/perspectives: sociological, psychological, physiological, emotional, spiritual, and metaphysical?

10. he says if he had a son who acted like him he would put him in a cage while he was doing drugs so he would be safe?

11. he feels lonely because he cannot converse with many people who understand his insight into the power and mystery of the energetic metaphysical world?

12. he takes a hallucinogenic drug that he's heard about but has "denied" himself from doing for months right in front of his AA sponsor during an AA meeting on his own back porch while his parents are home and becomes so psychotic he has to be hospitalized?

13. he jumps out of a moving vehicle and runs across four lanes of traffic to find his drug while his mom is driving him to a hospital?

14. he enjoys "tripping balls" so he can explore and enjoy other dimensions that aren't as cruel and cold as the third?

15. he has been homeless numerous times in the dead heat of mosquito biting summer and the dead cold of record lows winter for making bad decisions concerning drugs?

16. he refuses to let his mom help him manage his medication because he wants to have some control in his own life?

17. he has had numerous car crashes, all drug related?

18. he huffs in front of his mom, despite knowing it's a felony and knowing she'll kick him out again?

19. he is kicked out of college for inhaling a harmful intoxicant on campus although his biggest goal is to go to college to earn Nobel prizes in metaphysics?

20. he is booted out of the homes of at least six different families who loved him enough to try and help him but gave up because of his actions/addictions?

21. he makes many people question his IQ because he speaks so eloquently?

22. he has been in a psych ward 16 times since he was 16?

23. he is a people magnet because he intrigues almost everyone he meets with his insight, kindness, and humor?

24. he steals his father's bike and purposely rides into a car to try and kill himself although he wants most in the world to please his father?

25. he has been "working on his thesis for his PHD in metaphysics" since he was in high school?

26. he says that he could die today and be content because he has already experienced more than most people could in ten lifetimes because he's traveled through so many different dimensions and already has a clear understanding about the third dimension on Earth?

27. he is grateful for having nothing but one fork and the clothes on his back while living in a 10x10 one-room-with-no-kitchen-sink shithole apartment with a schizophrenic recovering drug addict/alcoholic that he met in jail?

28. he says he does drugs because he's anxious and the only place he doesn't feel anxious is at home--but then does drugs at home because it's the safest place to do drugs?

29. he says he does drugs despite having everything to lose because material things mean nothing, and the more he experiences nothing, the more he can expand his consciousness and reach enlightenment and keep the divine within?

30. he performs an articulate, beautiful, improvised speech when totally wasted about a family member at a wedding, inspiring everyone?

31. he steals his sister's prescription and mixes it with other drugs, stumbles around, denying anything's wrong, and then tries to jump out the window to kill himself?

32. he is an amazing thinker-philosopher-writer-musician?

33. he gives the shirt off of his back to another homeless person although that's the only one he has?

34. he believes he had to go to jail again because his subconscious mind told him certain inmates needed him to help them heal and reach the next level?

35. he wants to live in the Now and "Just Be" because "That's It"?

36. he believes that certainty and love are the most powerful energetic forces?

37. he never judges anyone for anything?

Brain train Tuesday, October 1

Can I train my brain?
I can train our brain.
Although it enslaves me,
I am its master.

Remember?

Indigo Child

The nurse caught my hand, squeezed it, turned me around to face her. I was being escorted through the locked door. The man with the key card stopped and said, "When you're ready, I'll be on the bench by the gate." He bowed, as if showing respect.

The nurse pulled me in, wrapped me with her whiteness and her warm, black hands. Her smile shined, a sun poking through clouds. "Honey, he's gonna be ok. I wanted to tell you that. And I wanted to tell you something else. He reminds me of an Indigo Child."

"I never heard of that."

"You go home and look that up, Honey. From what time I spent with your son, I can see it plain as day. He's a warrior, paving a path leading to higher consciousness. He's empathetic, charismatic, funny, to-the-point. He fights authority and every system out there. But I'm telling you, Honey, he's gonna be ok. He's smart, that boy, and he's gonna be okay."

She squeezed my hand again before the man swiped for the green light on the barred door.

For once, when leaving the mental hospital, I felt lighter.

Free to BE in Misery (K.t. and Aries)

You say you're sick of feeling like a science experiment because of the terrible side-effects of medication—the itchy rashes, the swelling of the throat, the weight gain.

You say you're sick of being a drone to society and would rather be an outcast than take prescription drugs that are harmful to your organs.

You say you'd rather feel pain than nothing at all instead of feeling like a zombie.

You say taking medication is a tricky thing.

I say, "Yes, it can be tricky, especially when abused or taken with other things."

You say you're done with medication, but ask, "Do you think I really need it?"

I say, "Yes, if it could help without terrible side-effects."

I say, "Yes, if it would help reduce your extreme anxiety which makes you throw-up every time you go into public."

I say, Yes, if it could help you be able to sleep and function for more than two hours a day."

I say, "Yes, if it would help you not feel compelled to walk into a burning trailer causing you to blister your face and singe your hair just because you wanted the experience."

I say, "Yes, if it could help you get your life back: enable you to go back to college, find and maintain a job, move forward and be happy."

You say you want to be free, just *be*.

I say, "There's a price to pay to be free in what many see as misery."

You say you'll pay the price.

<u>Do "be"</u>   *Friday, November 1*

What Aries said to me today:

You do you and I'll do me and together we will do "be."

Love it. Working on it.

To Whom It May Concern: November 16

I am Aries Wilde's great uncle and godfather, so I have watched him grow up. At times I have seen him interact perfectly with everyone from children to adults, forgetting that he has any problems. However, I know that his emotional issues can be quite debilitating, and I believe at this time he cannot successfully maintain a job, no matter what type it is. It's not that he doesn't want to work. He does, because he wants to feel accomplished and having a job is a way he can gain people's respect, and he wants that very much. But his mood changes quickly and often and although doctoring for years, he still hasn't been able to get it under control.

In the past, he was homeless off and on, sleeping at a friend's house on the floor, behind the bowling alley, or in the woods. Therefore, he couldn't possibly work. Currently, although living with a friend, he can't be depended on to arrive at a job when scheduled. Sometimes he has energy and other times he feels like all of the energy is drained out from his chest. This makes him feel sick, and when he feels sick, he becomes angry/frustrated and he can't accomplish what he wants (as he would say).

It's heartbreaking, because he is a very intelligent young man who wants to be a professor and teach psychology or metaphysics. He is also a talented musician and an excellent writer and friend.

I think receiving some aid could allow him to be in a healthier environment than what he's living in now. Hopefully if he has a place of his own to live he could focus on stabilizing his moods and move forward instead of being in the survival mode. Maybe he could go back to college and continue writing and playing music which could help him thrive as an individual.

Sincerely,

William Geist

A Mastiff on Our Mattress

Silence lies between us
like an old, lame dog--
a Mastiff on our mattress.
She circles, settles in,
and pushes us apart,
stretching stiff, bony legs,
poking paws into locked jaws,
sticking hips against sealed lips.
Doggie dreams dare her--her legs jerk and twitch--
but no whines, groans, or barks
escape from her lips.
Sometimes,
we burrow beneath her heaviness
to find each other's fingertips
or climb up and over Mastiff Mountain
to connect our lips.
Until we can speak without offending
what's inside our head
we'll deal with the dog until she's dead.

Meeting highlights:

-- _Live in the moment … Although I don't like many of the moments I'm experiencing lately, I know there's something to be gained with this practice. It will help me not focus on past pain and future worry._

-- _I am not responsible for the way anyone else feels … Why I feel so responsible for everyone I don't know. I don't need to take someone else's mood personally._

-- _Express my feelings instead of judging … I'm not a person who judges others, but I do judge myself. A lot. Meditation is helping me. I'm learning to observe, feel, and let go without judging. Also, I'm learning to express my feelings more. Typically, I keep everything inside. It's like I'm afraid to make waves. But what do I have to lose by speaking my thoughts? My opinions are as worthy as anyone else's, right?_

-- _Some things take care of themselves without me intervening … So true. I remember a few times feeling guilty because I did nothing, only to find out that a solution came about even better than I could imagine._

-- _I don't have to make a decision about anything right now … I like this a lot. It makes me feel lighter. Instead of feeling pressured right away in deciding what to do, I can say, "I'll think about it."_

E.d. *

I have no idea when my daughter's interest in Ed began, but it was probably in middle school when he flirted with her and every other girl he encountered. When she brought him home during her first semester of high school, I realized from her flushed cheeks that something was going on, but not enough to question the status of the relationship. She was, after all, a typical teen who walked around with that glazed-over-boy-crazy look, but she never cared to share about her relationships until her infatuation fizzled. Then, she'd complain about what a jerk he was for ignoring her and dating her now ex-best friend, or she'd explain how she'd moved on because he bored her beyond belief. So, I watched but said or did nothing.

Soon, however, I realized this relationship was different than the others. It wasn't a soft, puppy-love, but the hard, crushing kind. A twinge of worry shot through me, but, remembering my own high school days, I thought, *K.t., calm down. She's in high school. And she's crushing on sweet-talking, mesmerizing Ed. What girl wouldn't? If things don't work out and he breaks her heart, she'll be ok. She's been through so much. I know she's tough. And, as of now, she's having fun, taking it slow, and the hidden hand holding beneath the dinner table seems innocent enough.* So, I didn't worry …

Besides, Ed opened doors for my daughter--in more ways than one. He built-up her self-esteem within a few months of them going steady. My once shy-at-school teen now had everyone's attention. She lost weight, although she certainly didn't need to, changed her hair style and wardrobe, and looked absolutely fantastic. She exuded confidence. Although Ed had a bit of a bad boy reputation, he gave her total control. He helped her fit in and offered opportunities for daily thrills, enabling her to walk a bit on the wild side, which for her was comfortable—or I should say familiar. I never saw her so happy.

Throughout the school year, she squeezed more and more into her day, yet she still managed her time well. Before school she took care of her cats, dogs, birds, and rabbits; at school she aced all of her classes and became involved in art club and book club; after school she worked out with Ed, lifting weights in the gym and running five to ten miles daily. Then they completed homework together, pushing

138

for perfection. She loved being with Ed. He motivated her and did whatever she wanted. She was happy, and I was happy she no longer seemed depressed.

When summer settled in, I rarely saw her, and I saw no sign of him. Her summer job schedule made it impossible for us to connect. I was glad she had friends this summer, since the last one she had spent alone, but I started feeling a little nervous when she dyed her hair black and pierced her lip. I felt like I was losing her. I missed my girl.

I tried to pull her in, asking her to go to lunch, go shopping, stay home and watch a movie, but she had an excuse every time. I thought, *What teen wants to hang out with her mother when she has an exciting boyfriend?* I wanted to ground her to keep her at home but had no grounds. She had earned straight A's during the school year, was working a summer job, and had broken no laws or house rules (except the pierced lip). Ed always had her home by curfew, and it was obvious she loved him. When school started, though, things changed.

Suddenly she had the urge to purge all previous activities, so her going-out-every-night-after-work binge stopped. She restricted time with friends dramatically, to focus on her perfect four point. She restricted herself to her new vegan diet and a regimented work-out schedule, to keep in perfect shape. She became consumed with counting calories, pounds, reps, and miles. Obsessed, I'd call it as in the epitome of OCD. Although I was glad she was home, I became concerned when she was doing cardio workouts at 3:00 a.m.

But her diligence didn't last long. A month later she ditched the diet and dropped some of her seriousness and started indulging with Ed and her new-found friends. This off-on routine of binging, purging, and restricting went on for months. Actually years. Spending so much time with Ed changed her. She was different.

In the beginning of their relationship, she had the upper-hand. Now, she seemed to beckon to his every call. Later I learned about his controlling and manipulative behavior … and how sneaky she'd become to please him. I can't believe I was so naïve.

E.d. * (Continued)

In any case, I didn't like what I was seeing. She became wild and angry--unbalanced. I decided I had had enough. When I confronted her, said I thought Ed had become a bad influence, she told me not to worry because she was planning on breaking up with him—said he had become too controlling and she was sick of him.

Then she did it. She broke up with him. I was proud of her for being so strong. I felt incredible relief. But my daughter didn't. In fact she seemed worse. She paced and bit her nails and pulled the hair out from the nape of her neck. She kept telling me not to worry—said she would be ok—said being away from him was for the best. But it didn't take her long to cave in. At first she'd sneak away in the middle of the night to meet him in the woods. Then she started lying, saying she was out with friends when in reality she was with him. Later she wouldn't come home anymore on weekends, saying it was easier to stay on the other side of town with friends because it was closer to work. By this time she was eighteen, and I didn't have much of a say. She was living with him and I felt helpless.

Every time she came home to visit she would see the worried look in my eyes, so she simply stopped coming home. She never wanted to worry me. But she'd call, talk in an up-beat voice, tell me things were great, say things I wanted to hear. And I believed her. I believed everything was ok, because I *wanted* to believe everything was ok.

Months later she came home to visit. I gasped when I saw her, a dark, empty shadow. She had bags under her eyes. She was a bag of nerves, a bag of bones. When I begged her to get away from him, she promised me that she was definitely going to break it off for good this time. She said she truly didn't like what she had become. She said she now had the strength to leave him. She said she was waiting for the right timing, but it would be soon, so I shouldn't worry. She was so convincing that I truly believed that she meant what she said.

E.d. * *(Continued)*

And she did. She did it. Again. She broke up with him and came home. But he kept calling her, telling her she would never be able to find someone else that loved her as much as he did. Her obsession kicked in again. She fasted for days (because he called her fat), she ran twenty-five miles a day (because he said she had no muscle tone), she wore way too much make-up (because he said she was too ugly to be in public without covering her face). But, no matter what she did, she couldn't please him. Meanwhile, she lost more weight. She lost her hair in clumps. Her blood pressure dropped. She dropped out of college. Her heart skipped beats. She skipped all therapy and doctor appointments. She blacked out frequently, cut herself, and pushed away friends and family and food for him. She practically gave up her life for him. She no longer teetered on the edge of the danger zone. She plunged into the pit and stayed there alone in darkness, suffering, accepting no help, hopeless.

It took years. Many years. But despite dealing with irrefutable damage, she managed to slowly crawl her way back into the light by finally accepting treatment and learning to believe she could live without him. Despite knowing he seriously messed with her head, despite knowing he destroyed her life, despite knowing she didn't want to date him ever again, she can't get rid of him. He stalks her, living beneath her skin, in every cell of her body. He whispers in her ear that she's not good enough without him. He promises if she takes him back she can call the shots this time. It must be so hard for her.

After all, initially, it seemed, he gave her confidence. She blossomed into a beautiful flower. But he plucked her, leaving her rootless; pulled off all her petals, leaving her vulnerable; filled her stamen with guilt and shame, making germination a remote possibility. He left her as a frail, snapped stem …

*E.d. * (Continued)*

Maybe that's why, now, she's afraid to establish a relationship. She only likes the pursuit. She only likes the broken, the crazy. When anyone gets serious, she puts her barriers up and backs off. She wants to be in charge, but someone else to make decisions; to rescue, but be saved; to feel excitement, but experience peace. She wants to be loved, but is afraid.

I think it's because she still doesn't feel worthy. But she is. She is worthy of being loved. She is beautiful, inside and out. She is kind and smart and funny and amazingly talented. She just needs to believe that she is. My lovely Lavender needs to believe. She needs to believe in herself.

*Eating disorder

Money Doesn't Matter

Lavender sent me this letter to proofread before sending to the financial department at her college. She was so worried about wasting the money I paid for her classes. I don't care about the money. I just want her to feel better and stay healthy. That's all I want.

November 20th

To Whom It May Concern:

In October I was forced to withdraw from my classes. This decision was made after careful consideration with my psychiatrist and other healthcare providers. Over the course of the fall semester, several personal medical problems worsened due to the increased stress brought on by attempting to manage both my course work and my various diagnoses which were outlined in the attached letter provided by my doctor. Although I sincerely want to continue my education, at this time I feel it is best to focus solely on my personal medical issues. My past attempt to devote the time required to both my schooling and proper treatment was unsuccessful, as demonstrated by my rapid decline from being on the Dean's list to barely passing my part-time course load.

I am formally submitting this letter to further clarify my situation and request reimbursement for tuition, which was paid in full before classes began in the fall. Thank you in advance for your assistance in this matter. Please feel frce to contact mc at the number on the first fax page with any questions.

Sincerely,

Lavender Wilde

"Will you please give me a dollar so I can buy a beer?"

"Hell, no. I can't keep enabling you."

"I'm just telling you that I can feel something coming on. Before I just wanted to be away from people and have quiet time for myself, but now *I want something to happen.* If you wouldn't have come over just now, I would have made a bad decision. If I have something to drink, it will help me prevent myself from doing something really stupid. I just want to escape right now, but I don't want to go to crazy land and trip balls and see freaky shit and stuff. I'd rather do dxm to disassociate or huff, but my roommates won't let me do my choice of drugs. I don't know why because I don't judge them when they do theirs. They look like aliens with big black eyes. I don't like hanging out with aliens all day. They freak me out."

"Well, at least you can understand why they don't want you to huff. They don't like what you turn into with your shaking and sweating and creepy, deep voice."

"But look at what they turn into. I have to look at alien eyes all day, but I don't judge them."

"But you scare them."

"Well, then, maybe they'll understand how I feel every day. Anxious and scared. Why do you think I do drugs? And, think of Lavender with her eating disorder. How not binging or purging for two weeks would have been serious progress for her. Well, I haven't done any drugs for a couple weeks, so I'm making progress, too. At least I'm trying, but everybody only focuses on my fuck-ups and not my successes. I'm telling you if I have alcohol, I will be less willing to do other drugs."

"I don't know what to do. Yeah, I can buy you a beer so you won't do other drugs today, but what about tomorrow? I feel like I'm just prolonging your issues by giving you alcohol. What's going to happen if you get disability? Will you just consume yourself with drugs since you'll have money and you won't feel guilty spending it cuz it's yours? I just don't know why you do what you do …"

"I don't know. Maybe I was under a lot of stress in a past life and just need to rest this lifetime and do nothing and have no responsibilities."

"But you do want to do something with your life. You just said yesterday that you don't want to be like that homeless guy that you met under the bridge."

"Yeah, I'm not going to be like him. But now I feel so bad that I didn't help him. I know what it feels like to have burning feet and lead-filled legs when homeless. I feel like I should've at least gone and walked around with him."

"I understand why you want to help him. But you can't rescue everyone. You have to save yourself. You have to take care of yourself so you have energy to help others."

"I know but I just feel guilty for not helping him."

"Believe me, I understand. What are you going to do if you get your own place? I hope not invite everyone in who has ever helped you because you feel like you owe them."

"Why not? I do owe them. I'll be like Jack and just let anyone who is in a tough spot live with me. Or, I'll just tell people to get the hell away from me. I don't know. I need a car and a job so I can move forward with my life. But I've already lived more than most people. I've already done the hobby thing with making movies and doing back flips and I've already played my own music and written my own songs with lyrics and had awesome conversations with amazing people and done some cool spiritual work with Doctor S. I need to meet a girl. But I can't meet her without having a home and a car and a job. I'm a loser. I'm a fucked-up, lazy loser. No wonder Dad doesn't want to hang out with me. He hates lazy people."

"You're not a loser, Aries—"

"Yeah, I am. When I compare myself to you and Dad and Lavender and a bunch of my friends, I am definitely a loser."

"Well, ya gotta change something up then. You love Einstein. Heed his quote. You know the one where he says 'The definition of insanity is doing the same thing over and over, but expecting different results.' Stop doing the same damn thing over and over. Move on with your life already."

"It's too late. I already fucked up my life. I have nothing, and with my record I will never have anything because nobody will ever hire me. I'm fucked."

"Here. I gotta go. Take this two bucks so you won't do anything stupid and go buy a beer."

"Thanks. I totally appreciate you. You're a life saver. I love you, Mom."

"I'll talk to you tomorrow. Stay off the streets, OK?"

"I will. I promise."

Damn it. I caved in again. I'm such an idiot. I'm such an enabler. Here I am preaching to him to change things up and I'm stuck in the same pattern, too. God, help me. Well, it's just a beer. Maybe he won't melt his brain with duster today and get kicked out of the house he's living in and be totally homeless again. Instead he'll just do something legal and drink beer which messes with his esophagitis and makes him really sick. Wtf? I hate this. I hate that he's dealing with alien eyes, but if I let him come home, I might have to deal with duster face. I fucking hate this. What is the answer?

Waiting for the Other Shoe to Drop

Finally. Aries is in a residential rehab. Not an intensive out-patient program that never helped, but an in-patient, residential program. Finally, I can breathe. And sleep. At least a little. But I'm experiencing that feeling of anticipation. I'm waiting "for the other shoe to drop" as they say in my N.A.M.I. support group. Isn't that sad? Rather than finding peace and breathing easily, I'm still on edge. Well, the woman running the place said I can talk to him in two weeks, and it's only been one. I would think she'd call me if he left … although the other place didn't and suddenly there he was-- standing at my doorstep only three days after I dropped him off. So much for a thirty day program. How he got home when it was two hundred miles away I still don't know. Ok, Ok. Breathe. He's safe and sound and sober. He's eating and working the steps and sleeping in a bed, not under a bridge. He's not running from the cops or through fires. He's learning skills at an actual job where he is supervised. He's gonna be ok this time. He's gonna get better. He's gonna stay the entire six months and get placed in a job and live in a half-way house and be happy and healthy and healed and whole and proud of his ability to live on his own.

Three weeks later I received his letter:

> Hi, Mom. I made a new friend. He and I performed a skit in front of everybody at church and I really liked him. He was funny and smart and I could be myself with him. He was metaphysical so we could take our conversation to the next level. He earned a pass to leave to go to an AA meeting last night. We can do that after 30 days. He said, "Until we meet again" and hugged me hard before he went out. He was supposed to be back by 9:00. Well, he never came back. I was hoping he and I could do this together, but he's gone now. The guy he left with did come back though. But, he died last night.

Waiting for the Other Shoe to Drop (Continued)

In his bed right next to mine. From heroin. Today I found out my new friend died, too. He walked in front of a bus on purpose, according to the bus driver. Can't I please come home? How am I gonna get better here when people die from drugs in a drug re-rehab center and have no hope of getting better so they kill themselves? I need to be in a good environment. I need to be home. Please. Please, bring me home. Your son, Aries

I dearly love my cousin, Johnny. People used to call us "kissin' cousins" because we were inseparable. We looked like twins with our blond hair, blue eyes, buck teeth, and wire framed glasses. Unfortunately, Johnny's parents (my Uncle John and Aunt Lilly) died in a car crash when he was only five. Fortunately, my parents took him in to raise. All of my sisters and the neighborhood kids did everything we could to help him ease the pain of losing his mom and dad. We distracted him daily and had a lot of fun growing up playing kick the can, riding bikes, and swimming in our pool. He always made me laugh and was sweet and smart. He was my best friend and I could tell him anything.

Today, however, I don't want to talk to him. In fact, I don't ever want to see him again. I'm still trying to wrap my head around what's happened. I'm horrified and hurt and pissed and sad all at once. And I feel betrayed. I was trying to do Johnny a favor, but now I'm feeling like the bad guy. I'm sick of it all. And tired. I'm sick and tired of wrestling Johnny to the ground to get his keys when he's slurring, stumbling, and planning on driving. I'm sick and tired of feeling embarrassed when he gets really loud and in people's faces, telling the same story over and over. I'm sick and tired of seeing him already drunk when I go to visit him every Saturday morning for coffee. I thought he'd at least try to curtail his drinking around me, knowing what I've been going through. I know he's lonely and lost and needs a friend right now, but I'm going to have to stay the hell away from him for a while. Watching him drink himself to his death is even worse than watching Dad, and I can't take it anymore. I know alcoholism is an illness and all, but after his last shenanigans, I have to stay away. I can't try and save them all, for God's sake.

(Continued)

I thought when Johnny's best friend died in a crash caused by a drunk driver that he would think twice about drinking and driving again, especially since that's the way his parents died. I thought losing his house and wife and kids in the divorce, his teeth in the third accident, his freedom for a year, and his license for two years would jar something inside him to want to quit. But he still takes ridiculous chances.

We camped along the river with a bunch of friends all weekend. It was a rarity for us to get away, but Aries was in rehab and Lavender was staying at Ed's, so we took time to be with friends. I struggled with asking Johnny to go or not. Leo said not to, because he knows how disappointed I get and he just wanted to get away and not have to worry about anything for once. But I reminded Leo that it was Memorial Day weekend and for over four decades we had never missed celebrating it together to honor our veteran fathers and to remember Johnny's mom and dad. So, we both thought it would be good for all of us and asked him to come with us. I could kick myself.

Well, we cooked and ate like kings, canoed and enjoyed the baby eagles flying overhead, and played music and sang around the fire under the stars and full moon. We all had a blast. But I never saw Johnny sleep or eat or be without a beer in his hand. By Sunday, he reeked of alcohol and kept falling down into the rocks. And he left today, after drinking for fifty-some hours straight. I figured he would try to leave, because that's what he always does, so I rigged a deck of cards before he came, just in case, and conned him into playing a hand of poker before he tried to leave. The winner would get to drive his truck home. I thought it was a good idea because he knows I love his truck. And I didn't want to physically fight or argue about him leaving when he was intoxicated, like usual. Of course I won. I put his keys in my purse in my backpack and said he could

150

(Continued)

*ride with me or whomever he wanted, but I would be driving his
truck home. A no brainer, right? I was surprised that Johnny
actually acquiesced and I thought all was well. But he snuck into
my tent and took the keys and peeled out of camp before
anyone could stop him. About thirty minutes later my stomach
hurt terribly and I couldn't breathe and I threw up. An hour
later I got the call from a park ranger that his truck went over
the guardrail into the river. He was removed from his truck by
the jaws-of-life and taken by life-flight to a hospital at least
eighty miles from our camp.*

*I feel like an ass for not listening to Leo. Why don't I listen to
Leo? None of this would have happened if I didn't ask Johnny to
come with us. Maybe he'd be safe and sound at his apartment
in front of the TV. Why can't I let people deal with their own
issues? Why do I feel like I need to rescue them from their
misery?*

Damn it. Damn it. Damn it all.

Cutting

She eyed the blade--the razor blade.
She slid her fingers
along cold, smooth steel.

She gently picked it up
squeezed it between index finger and thumb
and with a quick slice made things real
below ten lines of scars on her thigh:

one purple
and scabbed
two raised
and red
three still
bright pink
four pale
but present
all ten at least
two inches long

Caught off guard this time--
she cut too deep, too wide--
she stared in shock
at the open fist-sized eye.
She couldn't stop the bleeding--
couldn't stop wondering

How did I let this happen? Damn it.
Now I'll need stitches and will worry Mom.

Cutting (Continued)

I felt so sad. I couldn't understand why my beautiful daughter would disfigure herself badly enough to need twenty-seven stitches. I thought she was feeling better after breaking up with Ed. But, obviously, I was wrong. Although I knew things were still bad and I needed to be vigilant, I didn't know the depth she dwelled in darkness. I was fooled by her and myself. After all, she was a great actress, and I was my too-optimistic self, trying to believe everything was ok and would stay that way.

Initially, the doctor at the emergency room pink-slipped her, planning to send her to the mental hospital, assuming she was suicidal. She pleaded with him. She explained that she wasn't suicidal—that she didn't mean to cut so deeply, certainly not deep enough to need stitches. She explained that she didn't cut out of a need to get attention or a need to be pitied. She cut because she wanted to relieve the mental anguish.

She explained later to me that cutting gave her something tangible that she could take care of concerning herself, something that she could control. She wanted to clean the wound, bandage it, watch it scab and scar. She wanted to help it heal. It was all part of her ritual—which always calmed her. Until now.

She and I both pleaded with the doctor and the nurse and the social worker to let me take her home, knowing that her last experience in the mental hospital was quite traumatic. Plus, there were no beds available locally, so she would have to go to the state mental hospital five hours away which was simply out of the question.

Cutting (Continued)

Finally, after some serious negotiating and a nurse admitting that "cutting" could be considered a "behavior" and not a threat of suicide, the pink slip was removed. I was allowed to take her home as long as she signed a contract that she agreed to be under my watch, take calls throughout the weekend from people working for the crisis intervention team, and go to her doctor's appointment the following week.

Two years later, I see Lavender sitting on the couch watching TV. She is tracing with her fingertips the many scars neatly lined up on her thighs and forearms. I imagine they remind her of times she wants to erase but can't yet escape from because of their prevalence.

All the fade cream in the world can't take the scars away right now, but hopefully, with time, each scar will fade. Until then, she has choices to make. She can face the scars, but not stay focused on them. Or not. She can accept them as part of who she was and is, but not assume they define her potential of who she can be. Or not. She can forgive herself and others she may blame for the role they played in causing their creation and move on, creating a beautiful life for herself. Or not.

I pray she has the strength to decide what's right for her highest good today.

When I asked Leo a few weeks ago if he would consider saving two hundred bucks a month he said, "Hell, yeah." I said if he could quit chewing tobacco, he could save that much on his health insurance. He said, "Well, I can try to quit, but you don't want to watch me. Because it'll be ugly."

And he was right. A week ago Leo was checking out some windfall from the latest storm and saw an innocent stray cat. As if possessed, he grabbed a long branch, lifting it up and back, ready to bash in the cat's head. Luckily, he tamed his feral hands and mind in time and said to the cat, "I could kill for a chew right now. It must be your lucky day." I wanted to stick a chew in his mouth right then and there.

When our neighbor saw all of this, he said, "For some people, quitting chewing tobacco is as difficult as quitting heroin. But you could get a prescription for the patch. Or if ya don't like that, you could try a pill."

Leo said there's no way he would take medicine to quit, but he was stubborn enough to keep trying on his own. The problem was that he lost all drive to work when he didn't chew, which really pissed him off, especially since we were always in the process of renovating. Besides, working was the only thing that kept him somewhat sane.

So, that was that. He didn't quit. But I wouldn't be surprised if he does someday, because he's stubborn, diligent, and enough of a tight-wad to try and save two hundred bucks a month.

155

Let It Be

"Let it be. Let it be. Let it be. Let it be. Whisper words of wisdom. Let it be."

One day while practicing this Beatles' song on my guitar I found myself crying, thinking of a conversation I had with Aries years ago. "Just be. Just be, Mom. Quit worrying about me and let it be. Do you know your worrying is actually hurting me? I can feel the negative energy. Why do you waste your time worrying?"

"I can't help it. I wouldn't worry if I didn't love you."

"Mom, if you think about it, that's ridiculous. When you worry, you're not living in the moment. You're wasting your time. You're sending me a heavy package of darkness and making yourself sick— all in the name of love."

"What am I supposed to do?"

"Send me a package of love and light instead. And let it *be*."

He was so right. I think of all the time I wasted worrying— precious time I'll never get back. I heard once that worrying is like rocking in a rocking chair. It gives you something to do, but it doesn't get you anywhere. It's certainly not proving to anyone that you care, despite what you think.

So, I've been working on it—not worrying, that is, and I've come a long way. I've had lots of opportunities to practice, just as we all do. Every time I catch myself consumed with worry, I think of my handsome son's comment. Now I send love and light to whomever/whatever I'm thinking about, and I let it be. It's certainly changed things for me.

That and This

When I'm drowned by deluge
or sucked dry by drought
and have nothing to give,
I have to remember:

It won't always be this way.

When my own garden flourishes,
I'll help anyone else in need
by offering my extra produce
and helping them water and weed.

Notice I said offer.

I'm finally learning
after many seasons
that some don't want
help with their garden.

I need to remember that.

And this:

I can't control the weather.

I Remember

I remember back in the day actually wishing Aries had a mental health diagnosis. Then I could say to people that he had an excuse for his crazy behavior of jumping off buildings, erratically slipping from one eccentric personality with a unique perspective to another, sleeping or not sleeping all day or night, or being totally "out there," as people would say. I didn't want to accept the fact that he was a drug addict like many people suspected. I never imagined he could be a bipolar drug addict. Be careful what you wish for.

I Praise and Give Thanks

The minister who is doing spiritual work with Aries calls me. We set up a time for them to meet. I tell Aries and he is excited. He says he is doing ok where he is staying. He says he can be loud without worrying and did some intense fight club moves with the guy who took him in, so he got out some rage.

I can't get a hold of Aries the day he is supposed to meet the minister. A storm has knocked out the power. I worry. And then I talk myself out of worrying. It takes practice. I move on with my day. I write and read. I am seized with worry a bit here and there, but I am not debilitated like I used to be. Every time worry over takes me, I envision white light and love surrounding Aries and I ask for divine guidance to lead him. And the same for me. Aries calls me the next day and says his phone was dead. He tells me he met with the minister to do some spiritual work. He says it was awesome. I am thankful I didn't spend my whole day worrying.

I meet Aries a couple of days later. He smells like a brewery, but he doesn't seem drunk. I offer to take him out to lunch, but he is paranoid of being in public, so I just drive him around and we talk. He says it's always so loud where he lives. The music—the shouting. He wishes he could have quiet surround him. He sees his probation officer coming out of a restaurant and has an anxiety attack. He apologizes for being a bad son. I tell him I'm trying not to judge. I say I know he's going to do what he wants and I am trying to do the same. I drop him off where he is staying and we hug and say, "I love you."

My heart breaks, but I pick it up and tape it together and go home and do life there. What else can I do? I've learned that I have to give him up to God. I pray. "God, I praise and give thanks that you protect and guide my son. I praise and give thanks that Aries can do Thy Will."

Pull the Plug (Song Lyrics)

Electrified. Petrified.
Wired wrong. Wired hot.
I think I'll blow a fuse if
I don't break the circuit loose.

Paralyzed. Freeze dried.
Stuck in a routine—
Electrocution. Persecution.
I can't stop worrying.

I need to pull the plug.
I need to spark the love.
Live without the fear.
Re-energize and realize
I don't need the tears.
Yeah, I don't need the tears.

Complicated. Frustrated.
Ja, ja, ja, ja, ja, ja, ja jarred.
Trapped with indecision.
Permanently scarred.

I need to pull the plug.
I need to spark the love.
Live without the fear.
Re-energize and realize
I don't need the tears.
Yeah, I don't need the tears.

Cut the line.
Zap the sap.
Totally break free, yeah.
Jumpstart the spark
for loving life … and jam the jolt of worry.
Jam the jolt of worry. Jam the jolt of worry.

Despite It All

Society says, "He's totally off his rocker."
He says, "I'm perfect--perfectly fine."
His friend says, "His mood changes so fast."
The doctor says, "I'd like to take things sloooooooooooow."
Since dealing with the system takes so looooooooooong,
I say, "Appreciate life; it's short."

Despite it all,
feel gratitude,
forgive,
love.
Learn your life lessons.

Then you can move on to higher things.
You chose those lessons for a reason,
so when they manifest, don't ignore,
because what you run from or resist

IS

so face them,
embrace them,
and be assured
they
are just
what you asked for,
despite it all.

Too Far Away

My daughter is
          too
               far
                    away …
In Paris, France, with a chance of
not being able to fly home to the states because
her boyfriend can't last an hour without alcohol.
How will she get him through customs
without being arrested? She's
stuck in a Best Western Hotel,
yearning to escape her hell:
the damned drunkenness
the blank stare
his stumbling mess
his "I don't care."
She wishes to rescue him,
yet wants to flee--
fly back to London alone,
needing to be free.
She sits with his booze locked in the hotel bathroom,
rationing it out so he doesn't have seizures.
She wishes she didn't call me,
regrets she got me involved—
sorry she's making me worry,
hoping things will be resolved.
I send numbers of the U.S. Embassy.
I call the hotel. But I am
       too
               far
                   away …

to help her escape her hell.

162

<u>*Don't beat myself up*</u>   *Nami Group   Wed., December 12*

Meeting highlights:

-- Don't beat yourself up for enabling, but be cognizant … I'm certainly aware but don't like being told by others. I beat myself up enough without their input.

-- You're not gonna be around forever to help … I want my loved ones to gain their independence. I don't want them to suffer like Dad did without Mom.

--Do whatever you need to do so you can sleep at night … I love this. I guess sometimes I have to do what I have to do despite what others think.

-- Don't get sucked up in the drama … I'm pretty calm, but sometimes I get pulled into mechanical mommy mode when emotions start flying. I always want to protect and rescue. I need to distance myself from the drama by walking away, breathing, and shifting gears.

--Ask the person struggling, "What are your options?" instead of trying to fix everything. Most people have pretty creative ideas about how to help themselves … I need to do this more often instead of assuming they don't know what to do.

Spring Equinox Brush Burning

On a snowy, moonlit night, we lit the last
of our winter's brush piles on the
first day of spring—
its earliest arrival since 1896.
Light emanating from our fire pit we call "First Snow"
revealed the beauty of our woods
with its sprawling glow.
In awe, I eyed the Tulip Tree,
Pin Oak, Oriental Flowering Crab,
Redbud, Beech, Staghorn Sumac,
Bald Cypress, and White Ash;
English and Black Walnut,
River and White Birches,
Holly, Loblolly, Wisteria,
Hemlock, Locust, Taxis;
the lovely Golden Thread Cyprus,
Swamp and Sugar Maples,
Apple, Cherry, Plum, Pear, Peach,
Pussy and Weeping Willows;
Douglas and Balsam Fir,
Buckeye and Horse Chestnut,
Juniper, Arborvitae,
Blue Spruce, Dogwood, Beechnut;
Gingko, Sweet Gum, Cottonwood,
Red, White, Austrian, and Scotch
Pines, multiple old-school Magnolias,
and the Norway Spruce stood watch.
Uniting our opposing natures
like the first snow in Spring,
the Equinox brought balance
to my arborist husband and me,
and with the light from our brush burning,
we could appreciate and *see*
thirty plus years of growing—
our forest through the trees.

164

The Sacrificial Lamb (K.t. and Her Cousin)

"How's Aries? I miss that guy. He's so fun to talk with, and, God, he's so frickin' smart. I wish I had his brains. He's the smartest twenty-year-old I know."

"I know … Believe me … I know. I've never met anyone else with his type of intelligence, and I had a lot of top-notch students throughout the years. But sometimes I wish he wasn't so smart."

"Why would you say that?"

"Because it's like a curse."

"Why would his intelligence be like a curse?"

"Because it's cursed him. Because he thinks so out-of-the-box, above and beyond the normal, he has a hard time fitting in. So, yeah, he's really smart ... and … he's also homeless."

"Oh, my God! The last I talked to him he was living with you, working, and going to college. He doesn't live with you anymore?"

"No. We had to kick him out … again."

"Again?"

"Unfortunately. We tried to have him live with us. Over and over. But every time he was home I couldn't breathe. I couldn't sleep. Leonard was a mess. His heart was always racing and he was so on edge. Lavender was afraid to come home--she was too afraid of what would happen next."

"God, I had no idea anything was going on."

"Yeah, not many people do. We've isolated ourselves pretty well. Nobody really knows what's going on. Half of the time we don't either. His issues and other stuff, too, have kind of imprisoned us. But we don't really want to go anywhere anyways. We don't want to deal with questions … and there's a lot of judgment. I guess you're gonna have that when mental issues and addiction are involved."

"Damn. I'm sorry. Can I do anything to help?"

"I don't know what to tell you. After sixteen in-patient stays in mental hospitals, multiple out-patient programs, and three visits to the "Sociological Experiment" (what Aries calls jail), I don't know what the answer is. Nothing seemed to help. No long-stay mental institutions exist anymore, but he wouldn't belong there if they did. The only way he can be forced to be hospitalized in a brief-stay psych ward is if he is homicidal or suicidal. When he was suicidal, the hospital stabilized him and then sent him home—or, now, in his case—to the streets. When he did come home though, he got caught in the same unhealthy patterns: he hung out with the wrong crowd, didn't take his psych meds as prescribed, and/or he took other drugs, too. He liked to experiment on himself--and when he was homeless it was even worse with no structure or routine. So either way, he made little or no progress. When he finally decided he was ready to go to a dual-diagnosis in-patient treatment center which could address his mental health *and* drug addiction, the center wouldn't accept him. It only would accept people who needed de-tox, and since his choice of drugs was not physically addicting, he didn't qualify. Also, the insurance company wouldn't pay a dime if he didn't need de-tox. They would only help pay for out-patient programs—so he went through many of those, but they weren't all day every day—they allowed him too much freedom—and he failed every one, every time. There are places called sober houses which are designed for long-stay drug rehab, but many won't accept people who are on psych meds because of the liability. And those places usually have at least a month waiting list and the person has to call every day until there is an opening so the place knows he is serious about wanting help. But even if the person is really serious, there is too long of an open window for a person with mental issues to stay dedicated to calling every day and getting in—especially if he is homeless and is an addict. And nobody else can call in for him. For any of these programs to work, the person has to *really* want the help. Aries wavers. It seems futile right now."

"So you're done letting him live with you?"

"Yes. There had to be a cut-off somewhere. Leo and I finally got on the same page after the tenth or twelfth hospitalization. I don't even remember anymore. In the past, I always begged Leo to let him come home from the hospital so he could have a chance of getting better. Although Leo thought I was babying him too much, he always acquiesced because he saw how tortured I was. We usually made some kind of contract that Aries would have to agree to in order to stay at home. Aries would be ok for a while, but he hated me bugging him about taking his medicine. We'd fight a lot."

166

"I'm so sorry."

"Me, too. It was hard because I was running myself ragged taking him to his psychiatrist, drug rehab programs, mental health court, counseling sessions, AA, probation meetings, whatever, but he wasn't taking anything seriously. He was more interested in learning how to play the system. And he was good at it. For a while. But things got way out of hand."

"So you're done trying to help him?"

"No. He's my son, and I'm not done. People tell me I should totally cut him off or he'll never learn. But I still buy him groceries and meet up with him and wash his clothes. I encourage him to take his medication, even though I'm not sure if he's ever been properly diagnosed--and I pay for his cell phone, so I can keep in touch with him. I try to help him as much as I can. But I'm done with him living here. I'm done being scared all the time, not of him, but *for* him. Of course I'm scared when he's not living here, too. It totally sucks. But it's better this way. Leo and I aren't fighting all of the time … and being away, I think, will enable Leo and Aries to heal and re-build their broken bonds. And Lavender, well, she does way better when he's not living here. It's sad to say, but we've had to make him move out to save ourselves. He's the sacrificial lamb."

"That's the saddest thing I've ever heard."

"Isn't it? I never in a million years expected my son would be homeless. It's heart-breaking."

"What can I do?"

"Call him if you want. He'd love to hear from his cousin. Tell him you love him. Take him to lunch. But don't give him money."

"But doesn't he need it?"

"Of course. But he doesn't know how to manage it. The last fifty dollars I gave him he gave to another homeless man, along with his only shirt, the one off his back. He does things like that—tries to help everyone but himself. Or he may buy drugs. He was or still is an addict. I'm not sure. I don't know if he can help himself, but I pray that he can. But, ultimately, it's up to him. They say he has to hit rock bottom. I pray his rock bottom isn't his death."

"I would have never known. He's such a great guy. So kind and sweet and smart and witty. I always thought he was a genius."

"As I said earlier, I think he's cursed. Just like Lavender and Leo. I think some people are too smart to be able to deal with this world and that's why they suffer so much."

"How do you cope?"

"I pray for them all. For Aries, I pray God guides him so he can gain insight to know what he needs to do and have the strength to do it. I pray to God that he can be the college professor that he wants to be. I don't know what else to do. I've tried to help him, but … I don't know how anymore. I sometimes think I care more about him and his future than he does. But I have to remember that it's his life-- his journey--not mine. I have to do what I have to do and so does he. What I have to do now is live my life instead of being consumed with saving his. So, every time I'm seized with worry or fear, which is a lot, I send a prayer—I ask God to send him light and love and guidance. I have to give him up to God and have faith. That's what it's come down to. It's the hardest thing I've ever done—letting go of my son."

"Wow."

"Yeah. That's what I say. Wow."

"Well, I'll pray for him. And for you and your family."

"Thanks. Thanks a lot. When I asked Aries specifically what he wanted me to ask for in my prayers, he said, 'Strength.' He said he knows what he has to do, but he needs the energy and strength to do it."

"Ok. I'll pray for energy and strength for him."

"Thanks. I appreciate that. I know he will, too."

It's time   _Monday, April 1_

Walking away
as far away as possible is my best strategy
to put life into my life. Whether it's wrong or right,
it's always a fight, a shot to the heart leaving a hole,
to leave alone and let my loved ones,
all struggling, fend for themselves.
After all, I'm the caretaker, the rescuer.
But things do change and it's time ...
to save myself.

You got this, girl.

One year later   _Tuesday, April 1_

April Fools! You thought you needed to walk away to save
yourself, not knowing you had everything within you to do the
work. And you thought they couldn't live without you. Well, you
never gave them a chance to prove to you or themselves that they
could until recently.
At least you're learning ... finally.

169

Ya Can't Make 'em.

Ya can't make 'em. Ya just can't do it.

Ya can't make 'em take the anti-psychotic
or not take too many pills for pain.
You can try your best to help save them,
but ya can't make them live life your way.

Ya can't make 'em go to the doctors.
Ya can't make 'em drink or eat.
Ya can't make 'em put down the bottle.
Ya might as well accept your defeat.

Ya can't change what they're made of.
Ya can't make 'em think like you do.
Ya can't stand to watch 'em waste talent,
but you can learn to take care of you.

You Could

You could always rescue them from nasty consequences,
let them do what they want with no rules or fences,
try to shield them from feeling deep despair,
or shove their issues in their face, proving you don't care.

You could have no empathy, be heartless, angry, cruel,
harshly judge those not like you as lazy, ignorant fools,
ignore them while they try to deal with their own strife,
or cut out the co-dependency eating you alive.

You could call their doctor who will prescribe pills,
the judge who'll acquit them or take away free will,
the treatment center who cannot force them to stay,
or their family who might send them away.

You could support them when they're trying to succeed,
help them help themselves get back on their feet,
give them guidelines when they can't think straight,
and fight for the rights they deserve today.

You could wait …
until the law locks them up
the psych ward ties them down
they're destroyed by others
or themselves
and are done.

You could pray…
for light,
an epiphany to bring change,
accept, forgive,
and love along the way.

You Could (Continued)

I still don't know what the answer is, but I do know it's time for me to focus on myself. Not to be mean or selfish, but that's how it is. Of course I'll help others if I can and want and they ask, but I'm no longer going to sacrifice myself along the way. Although our journeys may intertwine, I have my own path to find.

Our Transcendental Journey

We seek,
find,
and be the Light,
eventually,
because we all care
deep down
about our Transcendental Journey.

But it's a challenge.

Karma from us takes its toll
by dragging us through darkness
filled with fear of the unknown—

and we go on tangents,
because of thought seeds
previously planted.
Filled with guilt and lack of worth,
we put ourselves through Hell on Earth.

It's hard to watch

especially when we see in our eyes
the dark depths of our soul
from living arduous lessons
we chose to be whole.

But, we need to have faith
that Karma also pays
by embracing us with light and love and
showing us the way.

Our Transcendental Journey (Continued)

We need to check on our thoughts,
tend to All planted seeds,
and then fertilize the fruitful
and pull out the weeds.

We create the world we live in,
our Hell on Earth or Garden of Eden,
with the seeds we sow--
with thoughts we *believe* in.

We need to honor our bravery,
because we're all dealing
with Karma,
unfavorable planted seeds,
and living tough
lessons we chose
before incarnating.

We can wallow in self-pity
from these challenges above
or embrace free-will to change things up—
transcend, be light, know love,
and choose to understand:

Acceptance of,
Forgiveness for,
and Mercy to
All
are Key
when traveling through Time
on our Transcendental Journey.

Seeds of guilt and unworthiness   Monday, September 7

Some plants thriving in my family seem to stem from the deeply rooted seeds of lack of self-worth and guilt. Where did they come from? I wasn't raised with a suppressing religion and my family was pretty supportive, so I can't blame them. Have things rubbed off on me from others? Is it from this fast-paced, technological world in which we live? Is it from the constant bombardment by the media? Is it from the current collective consciousness? Is it from past lives? Why we carry around within us such negative thoughts I don't know.

But I do know I need to be cognizant of my thoughts because they can manifest into form. I want to create plentiful, healthy fruit to pass on for posterity.

The Fog (Song Lyrics)

When your imminent future hides
within mysterious fog at times
and uncertainty deters
when you're feeling so unsure,
have faith the fog will clear.
Trust your dreams are near.
Believe and blindly travel through.
Know that things will soon be true.

When low, thick, hovering mist silently manifests,
cooling, creeping, making a mystery out of all it blankets,
it often misdirects by whispering in your ear,
"You are lost, won't find your way, and your dreams aren't near.
Yeah, you are lost, won't find your way,
and your dreams aren't near."

But, you're not lost, you'll find your way.
Your dreams are here, and the fog will fade.
Weather's guaranteed to change,
so embrace this uncertain, cloudy stage
and ignore the fog today.

Instead listen to your heart. Yeah, listen to your heart. 2X

Have faith the fog will clear. Trust your dreams are near.
Believe and blindly travel through. Know that life is true to you. 2X

Have faith. Be true. Believe in you. 3X
Have faith to live your life as you.

Wow! It's been a long time since I've written!

I had to write because I love this date!

This is all that I have to say:

March forth!

Burning Fuel and Wearing Tires

At a conference about crystals, I learned that the feeling of guilt is made of the lowest frequency, totally opposing that of light and love. This makes sense to me, because when I experience guilt it seems like I'm dragging around heavy, dead energy. I feel like I'm shackled to a heavy ball and chain. I used to feel guilty every time I left the house because I was burning fuel and wearing tires, as Leo would say. I know leaving the house costs money, and I know Leo worries about money, because we've always been tight. He never wants to spend above and beyond our means, which I respect. But I've decided that going out and about to writers' meetings or visiting friends or helping out people I love is nothing to be ashamed of. Besides, the cost is minimal. So, I have stopped carrying around the weight of guilt to do the things I love. Well, at least I'm working on it. I have a need to connect with people whose frequencies radiate light, love, peace, and joy. There are a lot worse things I could be doing than burning fuel and wearing tires.

No Other Way for Me to Be (K.t. and Friend)

"I'm sorry I haven't touched base with you in a while."

"No worries. You've got a lot going on."

"How are you and your family? Even though we don't talk that much anymore I'm always thinking about you. I feel so helpless, though, and I don't know what to say or how to help and I worry."

"I understand that helpless feeling. Maybe you can do for me what I do for others. When I'm feeling helpless concerning someone, I imagine him or her filled with light and wrapped with love. Then I send a prayer. Here's an example. I'll say a prayer for you right now. 'Under the divine laws of grace, I praise and give thanks that Julie feels peaceful and helpful and receives whatever is best for her highest good.'"

"Wow. Thanks."

"You're welcome. Sometimes saying a prayer is all you can do. Also, remember things aren't always as bad as you imagine. I wasted a lot of precious time worrying, only to find out later that people I worried about were totally fine and even having the time of their life. I appreciate you thinking about us, but worrying is so wasteful. I'm so grateful I have you to spend time with. You help me by just being you."

"Thanks, my friend. You're always so positive."

"I've learned there's no other way for me to be."

Meditation Breakthrough

Wayward Thoughts:

a squeezing ravine
an iceberg drowning
a wind that rips up the dead
effaces my own
a swallowing forest
a sunrise deceiving
a fire that freezes
singes my soul

A lotus flower, pure,
welcoming, white,
warming with petals
and sunshine inside.

When wayward thoughts explore,
I accept, observe, let go,
still learning, yet now trusting,
they'll find Home.

We're Finding Our Way

Before going to our 30th class reunion, my husband told me he didn't even want to go anymore, even though we had already paid for our tickets and were looking forward to seeing friends from our tight-knit class. Why? Because everyone there would all be going on and on about their kids: "Well, he is graduating this year ... or he has an interview with blah blah ... or she just had an amazing offer ... or she just had her second baby and is doing really well ... or he is traveling to Europe for an internship this summer or ... whatever.

Well, we decided to go anyways and respond if questioned about our children with "Oh, they're finding their way."

We discovered we were not alone having kids who were still working on finding their way. In fact, despite being in our late 40's, we realized almost all of our classmates as well as their kids were still searching.

We're all working on finding our way. I pray we enjoy the journey.

Tricks of the Trade   _Tuesday, June 10_

Lavender told me that going to the eating disorder clinic probably saved her life! It's been years since she went, but it made me feel good that she told me. Sooo happy it was worth it!

Two years later ...   _Thursday, June 11_

Lavender admitted that she said what she said above to make me feel better ... said treatment didn't really help that much because she was so resistant, wasn't ready. She said, "What happened there is probably the same thing that happens to people who go to rehab or even jail: tricks of the trade were shared--not that I picked up on anything new. What also happened was a lot of competition, trying to be one up on everyone else when sharing stories--or should I say one down, since we were talking weight. Just so ya know."

It all makes sense. Although she had one of the best eating disorder psychiatrists in the world working with her at the clinic, she refused to give up the little control she had in her life to him.

Although Lavender doesn't believe the clinic was helpful, she always seems to be the one people come to for help with their issues because of her compassion and insight. I think her experience helped her gain skills that she isn't even aware of.

What I learned at the clinic was the following: Many people with eating disorders have traits of perfectionism, anxiety, and mood swings, and they certainly don't choose to have the illness. Oh! And they're very secretive, so I have to quit blaming myself. How could I have helped if I had no idea what was going on?

182

The Addict's Abyss

I look up
from the abyss I'm in
from where I
dwell in darkness.

Here I
dance with demons
daring and careless,
allowing them
refuge within.

Here I
fly with the gods,
riding on wings
through dimensions
no mortal has seen--
in worlds free from judgment,
sadness, hatred, and fear--
in worlds filled with peace
and love so rare.

But space narrows and darkens
after each trip,
the huge price I pay
for releasing my grip.

I look up and see light
but am filled with doubt
for what are the chances of me crawling out?

The Addict's Abyss (Continued)

I've burned all my bridges, lost all my friends,
and my family's lost hope in me again.
The light's far away,
my space, dark and small.
I look up and see white
but can't scale the wall.

So, I dance with demons and fly with gods.
It's all I know; besides, what are the odds
of climbing out? The challenge tempts,
yet faith is small; I'm filled with doubt.

I
sink
deeper.

But, then the light beckons me to climb out
and I'm tempted again
until my doubt
reminds me that although lonely and cold
my abyss offers freedom—wild and bold.

So, I choose freedom
to dance and fly
and I
sink
deeper
this time.

Darkness surrounds me.
I've lost the fight.
Why dare to dream that the tiny light
will fill me with inspiring life?

The Addict's Abyss (Continued)

Again, I dance and fly.
Again, I pay the price:
I fall even farther.
I can't breathe this time.

I've
hit
bottom.
I'm
Suffocating.
. . .

I have no choice.

I scale the wall.
I keep my grip.
Defy the odds.
Deny the trip.
I seek the light.
It's growing brighter.
I can make it.
I'm a fighter.

AAAAhhhhhhh

. . .

I look down into the abyss I was in—
where once I dwelled in darkness.

. . .

<u>Know Control</u>   Wednesday, August 20

Aries finally explained to me the meaning of the tattoo beneath his bicep that he got years ago. First, he read the two words: "Know Control," and then he covered up various letters along the way to explain its entirety.

<u>*Know control*</u>

> *because sometimes in life*
> *we think and feel we have*

_no_ control

> *until we come to the realization*
> *that we*

_now control

> *and actualize our lives.*

He's so deep, and he always makes me think. I pray he can practice what he knows.

Peace, Be Still (Song Lyrics)

Peace, be still. Peace, be real.
Feel the steadfast stillness wrap and
hold you tight.
Be the new life leader who
fights without a fight.
Bravely meet your demons
who dance throughout your night.

Be the light that waits for you.
Be the light that guides you through.
Be the light that lights your darkest night.

Peace, be still, so you can feel
the love within your heart that
ignites your light,
the love within your heart that makes everything all right.
Feel the peace of stillness
lift you through your life.

Be the love that waits for you.
Be the love that guides you through.
Be the love that lights your darkest night.

Our love is light,
so let's light our night
with love.

I'm so thankful for the opportunity of giving and receiving Reiki with my fellow Reiki Masters at our lovely bi-monthly healing circles. We focus on world and local issues, on intentions we've all put into a basket concerning our loved ones, and on each other. My personal intentions have focused on three b's during the last few sessions. Breathing, boundaries, and my book. I'm excited to say that my breathing is becoming easier and deeper; my boundaries, clearer and stronger; and the writing in this book, I hope, all of the above. I pray my finished project can someday, somehow, help someone, somewhere. If it doesn't, that's ok, too, because the writing process has certainly been a good release for me do some healing.

I love the five Reiki Principles. They remind me to take one day at a time. I think if everyone practiced these ideas the world would be a happier place.

Just for today do not be angry.

Just for today do not worry.

Just for today be grateful.

Just for today work honestly.

Just for today be kind to yourself and others.

~ Dr. Mikao Usui

Why I Love to Smoke

I love to smoke because it helps me breathe …
Ironically.
I
actually
stop
and
take
time
out
to
suck
life
in.

I savor
the moment.

But, I want to quit.
I convince myself
to suck life in
in other ways.

So, I take my plastic purple pen and
put it in my mouth.
I take a toke of
clean, fresh air
deep down, expand,
exhale despair.
…
Ahhhhhhhh

A Believer

Digging in rich dirt,
driving tractors through fields,
disking and cultivating,
planting, watering, harvesting,
processing produce, canning, composting.
A believer in the practical,
ready and willing to face the elements.
All in he was, is now,
a country boy, logical,
doing what needs to be done,
called to action
by solid ground.

Exploring spirituality
feeling what she can't see,
meditating and praying,
burning sage, cleansing energy.
A believer in the metaphysical,
open to face, embrace
unearthly possibilities.
All in she was, is now,
a simple girl, honorable,
doing what needs to be done,
called to action by a tug
on her ponytail when alone in a dark basement.

A Believer (Continued)

Grounding myself on Earth,
welcoming spirits of Light,
embracing beauty
substantial to ethereal.
A believer of Balance. Unity.
Gratitude. Love.
All in I am now,
a simple, country girl
doing what needs to be done,
called to action by Life.

To My Amazing Family (December 25)

What a ride we've ridden
with crazy, high ups, and deep, dark downs
and unpredictable twists jerking us around …
and we're still standing!
A bit dizzy at times
but pretty steady
relatively speaking
and gaining certainty
steadily
and I'd say
ready
to take a leap of faith
with Faith
in family
with Faith
in ourselves
to Be Who We Are:
those who embrace our loves
using God-given gifts
to create and share
with love--
up-lift.
We have Depth.
We have Height.
We have Width.
We have *Soul*.
I'd say
we're on a roll.

With Love, Love, LOVE,
~ Mom/K.t.

The Perigee Moon

Seemingly so close,
yet over two hundred thousand miles away,
the Perigee Moon
melts a perfect circle in
the black night and blue morning sky
with her huge, white beacon of light.

Seemingly so close, yet emotionally miles away,
we sit at arm's length in green chairs
along our tractor path by the tree lawn
in front of the cast iron wood burner that spits out
an eight inch wide and three foot high flame.

The fire flickers with a poke of a stick
and sparks and splatters burning embers
zinging and whizzing like
fireflies granting random wishes.

Closer than we've been for decades, yet still far away,
we watch the flames play while
the Perigee Moon peaks between branches of trees
still holding on to reluctant leaves
and shines with different intensities
through layers of grey clouds.

We, too, like the moon,
have experienced many cycles and shined
with different intensities through veils
clouding our fullness.

The Perigee Moon (Continued)

Yet, this date night sparks our love for each other
with a snap crackle clarity.
We move our chairs closer.
We hold hands.
We laugh a lot and thank God
the Perigee Moon reminds us of
the reasons why we fell in love.

They won't change until you do. Thursday, January 1

Over the years, I've been given all kinds of advice on how to handle the mental illness and addiction in my life. Everything from "You should rescue those in need" to "You should run for your life." What I've learned is I don't have to go to extremes. I just need to love myself and not lose myself along the way if I choose to help others.

That's why I agreed to see Johnny when he called and asked if I would meet with him. It's been three years since we've seen each other and two since we've spoken. I miss him and love him dearly and believe I can see him now without getting lost in his cosmos.

I've heard over and over that people won't change until you do. Well, I've changed a lot, so maybe he has, too. Or, since it's a new year, maybe he'll make a resolution. I'm willing, now, to find out.

We've Come a Long Way

Lavender and Therapist:

"Wow. I can't believe how much progress you've made since you did your first assessment with me seven years ago. You're not taking so many prescriptions, you're up to a healthy weight, you have lots of friends, you're going to college, and you're working. You're amazing."

"Thanks. Yeah, I've come a long way. Thanks for helping me get to where I am."

"Glad to be a part of it. People like you make my job worth it. As a therapist, I know it takes a lot of work to make progress, especially when you're dealing with tough issue like you've been dealt. But you didn't give up. You worked really hard to get where you are. Your strength and diligence are inspirational. I'm really proud of you."

Aries and K.t.:

"Wow. While going through my writing while working on this book, I can't believe how far you've come. Especially in the last year. I'm really proud of you."

"Thanks. Yeah, I've come a long way from back in the days when I was homeless and doing all kinds of drugs every day. Having a job for six months makes me feel pretty good and having my own place and paying my own bills blows my mind. A year ago I would never have imagined I'd be where I am now. I've learned a lot about what I don't want. I guess I have grown up a lot and made a lot of progress. Thanks for not giving up on me."

"I couldn't help myself. You're so worth it.

We've Come a Long Way (Continued)

Leo and K.t.:

"Wow. I was so frustrated today that I was leaping. I'm sorry you had to witness it."

"I'm not. I was in awe. And amazed you weren't swearing, kicking, and throwing things. Instead you were doing the vertical leap. I'm sorry I was laughing, but watching you leap was so damn cute. You've come a long way since we married. I'm really happy for you. I'm thankful you actually took time to visit friends while your glue was drying. You actually got out of the shop. That's big. Before you never would have shifted gears until the project was entirely done. I'm really proud of you."

"Thanks. Yeah, I guess I have come a long way. I used to feel way too guilty and anxious to stop in on some friends when I had some down time during the work day. But I finally did it and am glad, because I had a great time. I have to do that more often."

K.t.:

Wow. I used to curl up in the fetal position and cry all the time. I'd also worry myself sick and isolate myself, believing nobody understood. Now, I re-route my thoughts when I'm worrying and embrace the world and people around me. I've found the free-spirited self I lost, smile a lot more, and truly believe again, as my Dad used to say, "Life is beautiful." I am grateful I've come such a long way.

197

Attachments

This year I promised myself that whatever I hadn't used in decades I was going to put out for the annual garage sale and not bring back in, and whatever I took down from the attic for the sale I would not carry back up. "I'm done," I said. "I'm done with storing stuff I'm not using. Plus, purging can be a healing thing—good for the soul." I was adamant.

But, when the little old lady wanted to know the price of the blue Atlas pint mason jar that Leo said was part of the three-piece set worth thirty dollars, I said, "I'm sorry, but it's part of a set."

"Oh, darn it," she said. "I just really wanted that little one to show off on my kitchen counter."

Seeing the forlorn look in her eyes and wanting to sell everything in sight, I said, "Okay. It'll be five dollars."

She picked it up, thanked me, and kissed the jar, exclaiming, "What a beauty. Thank you so very much, my dear."

For a moment I was happy, knowing she appreciated its vintage charm, but then sadness seized me. What would the other two pieces do without their third? And why wasn't I showing off those jars on *my* kitchen counter? It took me awhile to console myself, but I kept thinking about my goal. Besides, her gratitude made my day and I certainly made hers.

My next customer was the cute neighbor girl who asked the price of my hippie dress--the multi-colored one with stars, moons, and peace signs. The one with a silk lining that made me sweat (and I don't sweat). I said, "One dollar."

She smiled, holding it up to her shoulders, and she twirled around the yard, saying, "It's so light and airy and free." For a moment, I remembered dancing in that dress, feeling her joy. I suddenly wanted to change my mind and say, "Oh, sorry, I made a mistake. That dress isn't for sale." After all, that dress was a part of me, had been with me since the seventies, and knowing that it wouldn't be there in my closet made me melancholy. *But, letting go is healing and good for the soul*, I reminded myself. "You'll look beautiful in it," I said. We both smiled.

Attachments (Continued)

A young man approached me. "Excuse me," he politely said. "What's the price of this pink purse with all the beads on it?"

I paused, thrown off a bit. I recognized his face but couldn't place him. "Why do you look familiar?" I asked.

"Oh, I delivered a pizza to you before. I thought this might make a nice gift for my girlfriend if it's not too expensive."

Without hesitating, I said, "It's free."

"Oh, wow. I didn't expect that. Really, thanks a lot!" As he left to deliver his gift to his girlfriend, I suddenly felt like dancing.

The rest of my garage sale was filled with saying goodbye to many more items and hello to more attic space, but not everything sold, of course. I was thankful Mary and Robby stopped over with Lucy, their new friend, just in time to help me clean up. They asked me where I wanted to put things. Sticking to my guns, I said, "Nothing goes back into the house. I'm donating it all." So, we packed everything into the truck: Tupperware with missing lids, Beanie Babies, Sesame Street and Austin Power videos, Dr. Seuss books, one crutch (don't ask), a music box with a ballerina on top, a box of encyclopedia Britannica, a never-used tread mill, a fish tank with colored pebbles and rocks, assorted picture frames, at least a thousand hangers, jigsaw puzzles, a Kodak slide projector, a black rotary phone, and an outdoor mat saying "Welcome Home!"

Everything was packed. *Except* for my mom's twenty-six piece crystal punch bowl set. True, its ladle was broken and its glass cups were ridiculously small. I never used it. In fact, I couldn't imagine ever using it. But I couldn't bear to see it go, so I set it in the foyer rather than carrying it back up the gazillion steps to its spot in the attic. I decided I was allowed to think about its fate. One free pass.

Finally my friends and I could relax on my back porch out of the hot sun. While pouring lemonade, I commented that I was surprised at my emotional attachments to things. Lucy, whom I just met yet felt a connection with, said she recently learned to let go of things.

199

"I left everything I loved in Texas," she said, "except for the clothes on my back. That's the only way I was able to get out of an abusive relationship. Then, after acquiring more stuff when I moved up here, I lost everything when my apartment complex caught on fire. That's why I try not to get attached to things anymore. But, people, well, they're different. They're worth getting attached to and they're worth missing when they're gone, as long as you can still move on, somehow, without them. Well, that's my story and I'm sticking to it. May I use your bathroom?"

"Oh, sure. "It's through the back room and to your left."

"Do you mind if we go take a walk in your woods?" asked Mary.

"Go for it," I said.

After Mary and Robby walked out back, I thought about all of the loved ones I've lost and how I've learned to cope. I thought, then, it *should* be a piece of cake for me to let go of material objects.

When Lucy came out, in spite of the heat, she was rubbing her arms. She had goosebumps.

"Are you cold?"

"Um, no. I usually don't say anything, but since you seem kind of open and we've been talking about emotional attachments, I'm gonna ask you straight up, "Do you know you have a ghost living in your house? I think it's attached to your antique." She was pointing into the back room where my husband displays his vintage barber chair.

"Really? I thought we got rid of all of the ghosts a couple years ago. Except for one."

"Have you always had that chair in there?"

"Actually, my husband just brought it into the house about a month ago. Our friend whom we fondly called "Floyd the barber" passed away. His kids gave Leo the chair because they knew he appreciated old things and would give it a good home."

"Well, that would explain why you didn't know about this ghost. He isn't sitting in the chair, but he's certainly attached to it. It's weird. He's kind of crouching behind it like he's hiding."

200

Attachments *(Continued)*

"I hope it's not Floyd hiding from a disgruntled customer seeking revenge for the Bozo haircut," I chuckled. Lucy laughed, then asked, "You said you got rid of some ghosts but still have one. What's the story?"

"A couple of years ago a student of mine told me about a woman she called Ghost Lady. I called her and she came over. While going through the house, Ghost Lady discovered that one ghost was attached to the magnolia needle point chair we got from an antique store. Another was attached to the vanity with the huge oval mirror in the bathroom. There were other ghosts, too, stirring about, especially in my son's room. Ghost Lady said they were disturbed by the chaos and changes due to our renovations. In any case, using sage, holy water, and prayers, she made it possible for them to let go by leading them to light. They all left except for the woman in the bathroom wearing her dress with its high-necked, buttoned, lace collar. Ghost Lady couldn't convince her to leave—said she stayed seated, brushing her brown hair, obsessed with looking at her reflection in the vanity's mirror. Ghost Lady assured me, though, that she wasn't hurting anything. Since my children started sleeping better after Ghost Lady did her thing, I didn't worry. So, I assume she's still there."

"Would you like me to see?"

"Sure, if you don't mind."

When we walked through the backroom, after passing the barber's chair, her goosebumps returned. As we walked up the stairs to the guest bathroom, she said, "Oohh … now my neck is all tingly. The barber is following us. Maybe he wants to meet her, too."

At the top of the stairs, we could see the bathroom door was open. "That door is usually closed," I said.

"I hope she's still there" replied Lucy. I had mixed feelings, but I'd feel better if she had gone to the light where she belonged.

The woman in front of the vanity mirror was not there.

"She must've been ready to move on," said Lucy.

As we explored the rest of the second floor, she found no ghosts. "What's behind that door?" she asked.

"The stairway to the attic." I opened the door, felt around for the light switch, and led Lucy up to the top of the steps. We paused to take it all in.

"Wow. There's a lot of confusing energy up here," Lucy said. "Especially over there." She pointed to the section I had stored the belongings of Aries.

Silently, I prayed that Aries was of sound body and mind. Slowly, I scanned the attic filled with a lifetime of possessions, reviewing all the stuff I'm still holding on to. I thought about ghosts unable to detach from their things, unable to be with the light. I took note of the empty spot between my old college typewriter and the bassinet filled with favorite toys and stuffed animals. Then, I said, "Let's get out of this heat."

When Lucy and I walked downstairs to the foyer, I saw Mom's punch bowl which once filled a now empty spot in the attic. I decided right then *not* to take the bowl back to the attic.

"You know, I think I'm going to plant violets in it," I thought out loud.

"In what?"

"Oh, the punch bowl. African violets were my mom's favorites. They'll look beautiful in it. If I'm going to be attached to things, I might as well make sure they remind me of good memories and the people I love."

"I guess everybody has their time for holding on and letting go," Lucy said.

"Yeah, and now I know I can let go … and will let go … when my time is right."

I Used to Wonder …

I used to wonder. Would things have been better if I'd never had kids with Leo or left him when the kids were young instead of toughing it out and working on the marriage?

I used to wonder. Would things have been better if we agreed on how to raise children?

I used to wonder. Would things have been better if I'd breast fed longer, was a stay home mom, had the kids farther apart, taken the kids to different day cares, played more with the kids instead of always working, or taken them to church more regularly?

I used to wonder. Would things have been better if we hadn't bought the Queen Anne in the city or the farm house in the country or not lived in chaotic construction zones while renovating them?

I used to wonder. Would things have been better if I'd known that we had ghosts attached to our antiques, that they got riled up when renovation or change happened, and that they could be encouraged to find the light by using prayer?

I used to wonder. Would things have been better if I'd lain with Lavender *every* night when she couldn't sleep or allowed Leo to "beat" Aries because "That's what Wilde boys need"?

I used to wonder. Would things have been better if I had known about all of the drugs so easily available to teenagers in our small community, pushed the kids to be more involved in school activities, been more active in my kids' school and less active at the school in which I taught?

I used to wonder. Would things have been better if I'd listened to Leo and not let the doctors put Aries on any prescriptions or sent Aries away for two years' dual diagnosis treatment even though insurance wouldn't pay?

I used to wonder. Would things have been better if I'd found all homeopathic treatments for both kids instead of taking them to psychiatrists for prescription drugs, taken them to different therapists or psychiatrists, forced them into more counseling and support groups?

I used to wonder. Would things have been better if I'd known more about the devastating effects of mental illness and addiction, detected their signs earlier, and intervened before I did?

I used to wonder. Would things have been better if I'd only tried harder?

Now I wonder … how did I manage as well as I did with all that we had going on?

I finally realize I can't beat myself up, blame myself, or isolate myself anymore. I know people may judge me and mine for how we handled things, but we were/are only humans being human, reacting out of love or fear. I now know I did the best I could with what I had at the time. I learned to take care of myself. I joined support groups which helped me gain insight, learn boundaries, and reach personal goals. I practiced yoga, learned to meditate, read self-help books, and became a Reiki master. I never stopped loving my family even when they hated me for "caring" too much. It's been a wild ride, yes, but it was/is our Wilde ride, and I have faith, with light and love, we'll make it through.

Holding On

Hold on, hold *on*, *hold on*! That used to be my main mission in life. However, I learned that's not always possible while riding a rollercoaster with manic highs, dark lows, and unpredictable twists.

I've discovered the only things I can hold on to are memories. While my mind still allows me to keep them safe, I reminisce about favorite moments such as these: Johnny and I pretending my dog's house was a boat that took us on many adventures. Rolling out noodles with my mom and great-grandma on the walnut round table while smelling homemade rolls baking. Philosophizing with Dad on the blue couch in front of the fire place. Falling in love with Leo while cross-country skiing in what looked like melted marshmallow land. Taking our couch camping to the top of a mountain and sleeping in the apple orchard under the summer stars. Finding a perfect heart shape in the center of a sugar maple leaf *and* a fossil rock on the same day while hiking down a ravine. Leo and I both weeping with joy when welcoming to the world our bear-pawed Aries and our piano-fingered Lavender. Camping out at Gramma and Grandpa's with the entire family to celebrate everyone's birthday in one weekend. Singing James Taylor's "You've got a Friend" with friends inside our barn lit with candle light during a winter snowstorm.

In order for me to make these memories, I had to *be* in the moment, not trapped in past sadness, future fears, or focused on things I couldn't control. I don't know how the rest of this Wilde family's ride will go, but I do know the most important thing I've learned about holding on ... is letting go.

ABOUT THE AUTHOR

Reiki master and retired educator Tam Polzer loves creating and giving presentations. "Nature's Way Journaling" showcases her photography and reflective narratives to inspire creative writing. "Do You Believe in Angels?" informs and shares her personal angelic encounter. *The Kitchen Fairy*, a heart-felt novella about the strength of a family's love, is available on Amazon. She has also been published by Crisis Chronicles Press and Writing Knights Press and can be seen in their *Hessler Street Fair Anthologies* available at Mac's Backs in Cleveland Heights, Ohio. Tam shares her writing at Words and Wine, a monthly poetry reading, and practices Reiki in her home. She loves hiking, biking, hauling brush, practicing yoga, and spending time with her adult children. She lives with her amazingly talented artisan husband and two cats in northeastern Ohio. Learn more at polzersprojects.com.

How many faces
do you see in
the Reflections
from the Wilde
Side's façade?